When Babies Read

When Babies Read

A Practical Guide to Help Young Children with Hyperlexia, Asperger Syndrome and High-Functioning Autism

Audra Jensen

Foreword by Peter S. Jensen MD

Jessica Kingsley Publishers
London and Philadelphia

First published in 2005
by Jessica Kingsley Publishers
116 Pentonville Road
London N1 9JB, UK
and
400 Market Street, Suite 400
Philadelphia, PA 19106, USA

www.jkp.com

Library of Congress Cataloging in Publication Data

Jensen, Audra, 1972-
    When babies read : a practical guide to helping young children with hyperlexia, asperger syndrome and high-functioning autism / Audra Jensen ; foreword by Peter S. Jensen.-- 1st American paperback ed.
        p. cm.
    Includes bibliographical references and index.
    ISBN-13: 978-1-84310-803-0 (pbk. : alk. paper)
        ISBN-10: 1-84310-803-8 (pbk. : alk. paper)   1. Dyslexic children--Education. 2. Autistic children--Education. 3. Language arts--Remedial teaching. 4. Reading--Remedial teaching. I. Title.
    LC4708.J46 2005
    371.91'44--dc22

                                      2005016785

British Library Cataloguing in Publication Data
A CIP catalogue record for this book is available from the British Library

ISBN-13: 978 1 84310 803 0
ISBN-10: 1 84310 803 8

Printed and Bound in Great Britain by
Athenaeum Press, Gateshead, Tyne and Wear

Contents

Foreword

Only a few years ago did I learn from my nephew Dave and his wife Audra about the troubling symptoms that their precocious two-year-old son Isaak was showing. Isaak's acute over-fascination with letters and words, his gaze avoidance with his caring family, his temper tantrums when his routines were interrupted, and his spontaneous ability to sing the alphabet song backwards—to my child psychiatrist's eye, all these characteristics suggested something more ominous than simple precocity. For Audra and Isaak, I arranged an evaluation with my colleague Geri Dawson, an autism expert whom I had gotten to know and to greatly admire while I served as the Associate Director of Child and Adolescent Research at the National Institute of Mental Health. Before long the definitive diagnosis of autism was made.

"For Isaak, you must become THE expert," I told Audra, knowing the terrible lack of resources most children receive. "Don't settle for less than what he needs. Even though all the evidence isn't fully in, get him into intensive ABA programs. And if you need to, be prepared to get a lawyer, who will write letters on his behalf to the school or early intervention programs. Learn what his rights are in educational law, and go out and get it."

No lioness ever defended her cubs more fiercely. Though our initial phone conversations were probably no more than one-half hour (I lived at the time in Washington DC, and Audra, Isaak, and Dave in the Pacific Northwest/Seattle area), what an amazing, marvelous transformation overtook Isaak's parents, particularly Audra who had all the day-to-day responsibilities for arranging his care. She quickly absorbed and evaluated all new information. She learned to not take "no" for an answer. In her small county public school system, she led successful efforts to transform early intervention programs and services available to youngsters with autism and other widely misunderstood pervasive developmental disorders.

Becoming increasingly expert, she learned when to go with the standard medical advice, and when to trust her instincts. Yes, all of the therapists, doctors, and educators knew a lot about autism, but she lived with Isaak 24/7. Audra understood that she was (and is) the expert about Isaak. Never bull-headedly, and only after considering all the facts and drawing upon her own experience, fortunately for Isaak and for all caregivers and educators who will read this book, Audra followed her instincts, and in the process discovered new keys to help her son use his precious but overgrown language abilities to move forward in areas of social functioning.

For those readers who benefit from Audra's wisdom, insight, and experience with hyperlexia, I would also encourage you to read between the lines, and learn the other lessons she has to teach. Learn all you can about your child's condition. Become expert. Look for the keys for that which works for your child, and don't stop until you have found them.

Peter S. Jensen, MD
Ruane Professor of Child Psychiatry
Director, Center for the Advancement of Children's Mental Health
Columbia University

Preface

You are unique, and if that is not fulfilled then something has been lost.

Martha Graham
(American dancer, teacher, and choreographer, 1894–1991)

He's sitting next to me on the couch now, reading a book. He's not even six yet. He thinks he's big, but he's still my baby. He turns to me. "Can I tell you a secret?"

"Sure."

He climbs up to me and whispers in my ear, "I love you." He pats me on the head before he jumps down and runs off.

He may never know how much that means to me, not until his own child is locked away in a world of written words.

It is now two years later and I am finally coming to an end of this writing process. When I look back on these past years, it feels almost like a dream. There were days in the early years that I didn't want to get out of bed. It was too hard. It was too much work. I just wanted to sleep the year away. Maybe the next year things would be better. But I did get up, and the next year, things *were* better. Time passed. He progressed. I learned. I now am extremely grateful for those challenging years because *I* grew. It was all worth it. I was "schooled" by a little boy with autism.

In this book, with the exception of the definitions, I do not separate autism from hyperlexia. This does not mean that I believe that autism and hyperlexia always coexist. There are children with hyperlexia that do not have autism. From my experience, however, the majority of kids who have clear hyperlexia also do have some level of pervasive developmental disorder (autism spectrum disorder). It has also been documented in at least one research article that between 5 and 10 percent of children with autism also have hyperlexia (Burd and Kerbeshian 1985). For the purposes of this book, I will not separate the two, for whether your child has hyperlexia with autism or hyperlexia without autism or autism with advanced visual skills, the strategies suggested in this book do not differ. The key is to learn your child's learning style and to use that advantage to help him overcome other challenges.

In the book, I refer to the child with hyperlexia as "he." Although many children with hyperlexia or autism are girls, the majority are boys, and for simplicity purposes, I use the masculine pronoun.

The point of this book is to give you ideas. There is no set formula, no magic potion. This will, it is hoped, be only one of many references that can be used to customize a unique program for your child.

Acknowledgements

I wish to acknowledge the hyperlexia community of parents who have given me ideas and made me realize I wasn't alone. Special thanks to Uncle Peter who got us started on the right road and helped us all along the way.

Thanks to all the teachers who have seen Isaak as "just another kid," who were not only accepting of him, but loved him and saw him for the amazing person that he is. Thanks to the speech and occupational therapists and ABA consultants and tutors. Special thanks to Northwest Behavioral Associates in Kirkland, WA, for being our program manager all these years, and who dedicated hours and resources to help Isaak live up to his fullest potential. Many of the ideas outlined in Chapter 8 were adapted from their programs. They can be found at http://www.nba-autism.org.

Thanks to supportive friends who, over the years, have made this journey more bearable. Thanks to Allyson and Lizz for lending a shoulder to cry on and another one to laugh on. Thanks for giving me a break on occasion despite my protests. Thanks to Chris for journeying down the same path with me. May our lives always be so close.

Thanks to parents and siblings who have shared our lives, who have felt the joy and despair with me. Thanks for making me laugh.

Thanks to Maggie for being the sister that Isaak needs. Thanks for your cheerful attitude. You light up the room when you come in. Thanks for your ability to accept others, to see all people as worthy of your friendship.

There are no sufficient words to express my gratitude to Dave. I could not have survived the journey without you. You are my rock. You are my grounding. You are a loyal and dedicated father. You step in at a moment's notice and achieve all that needs to be accomplished.

None of this would have been possible without Isaak. You have taught me more in these eight years than I ever could have learned in a lifetime without you. Thanks for your innocence, for your pure love. Thanks for showing me what it is to be without guile. Thanks for your enthusiasm for things I take for granted—silly sounds, knock-knock jokes, and math. Most of all, thanks for teaching me to love unconditionally.

Chapter 1

Something about Him

"There's just something about him." It's a phrase I became accustomed to hearing from the time he was small. And there truly is—just something about him.

He would sit and look at books for hours. He would turn the pages so gently. He would look at the words on the page more than the pictures. He was only a year old. He could identify many letters of the alphabet. He didn't smile or laugh much—only when he was rough-housing or playing with his letters. He appeared almost deaf—not responding to his name.

Then he was 18 months old. He could line up the alphabet from beginning to end. He could identify all the letters on sight. He could sing the alphabet song—backwards, no less. Numbers began to matter to him. He could count a large number of objects. He didn't seem interested in other children. There was no child-like anxiety of strangers. He began to have violent tantrums for no obvious reason.

At two, he spontaneously began to read. He was obsessed with it. He wanted to line up plastic letters all day long. He had never called me *Mommy* or used any other word consistently. His days continued to be flooded with tantrums and rituals. People were furniture. Indulging his obsessions of letters and numbers was often the only thing that made him happy. That, and reading. More and more reading.

It was a few months after his second birthday that we sought expert help. He was given a diagnosis of autism and hyperlexia. I knew from that first day that we would fight it in the same way we would if he were diagnosed with leukemia. We would fight and work and battle the "cancer" in his brain. We could see that the autism was taking over. It was eating up all the normal, happy elements of his personality. The more time went on, the more he fixated on his obsessions and the less he interacted with people. He needed to regain a developmental balance. Yes, we had to fight this.

By the time he was two-and-a-half, we had a full program running for him. Half the day was spent in an early childhood special education program. The other half of the day he had speech therapy or occupational therapy or home tutoring. He worked from the time he woke up until the time he went to bed.

The first few months were hard. He was a fighter. He spent most of his time screaming and resisting any intervention. We persisted. For good behavior or compliance, he was awarded with a letter sticker or stamp. We sang the alphabet song. We wrestled around. We expected a lot out of him, and he began to respond.

As he began to settle down and make progress, we began to use these unusual skills that he possessed more and more to teach him additional skills. He was still not using any language to communicate anything, so that was our first goal.

Isaak was attached to his sippy cup. He would regularly go to the kitchen and whine. I had unsuccessfully tried to get him to say the word *drink* and had even tried to get him to simply point to the fridge. He didn't understand any of that. I usually just gave him a drink and patted him on the head.

Isaak could read the word *drink* and I knew it was the one thing which he desired above all else. One day, I waited for that familiar whine. I was in the kitchen, at the refrigerator, index card in hand that said *drink*.

"You want a drink? *Drink.* Say *drink*." Whine, cry. "Say *drink*." I handed him the card. More crying. He looked at the card.

"Drink," he read, and then he started crying again. I saw no light bulb. I immediately handed him the drink. Then, it clicked. He didn't say anything, of course, but I could see it in his face and in his demeanor. I can only imagine him thinking, "The words actually *mean* something." This was more than labeling. This was *communicating*.

I made a set of index cards with common words he would need throughout the day. Words like *sit down, stand up, sing, read, night-night, bye-bye,* and *eat* were in the set. I laminated them and put them together on a metal ring. I called it the Read-and-Comply game. When playgroup was going to song time, I'd have him flip to the *sing* card and then prompt him to go to the song circle. *Sit down* would be next, and I would have him read it and then sit down. Snack time would elicit the *eat* card and bedtime, *night-night*. It wasn't a difficult concept, but for a two-year-old with no communication skills, only reading abilities, it was a rather peculiar thing to be teaching. Isaak learned his first communication words through that little card book. That would take us into a whole new, unconventional way to teach him language.

Soon it was time to teach him to use simple sentences. I had an index card that said "I want" on it. When he started whining for something, I'd hand him that card and he'd read, "I want" and then finish it with "banana" or "drink" or "book." He was making his first sentences. I'd show him a picture of someone doing an action and I'd hand him the prompt, "_____ is _____" and he'd fill in "Boy is swinging." He was using sentences for the first time in his three years.

After I started working with him, I began to see that I *could* have expectations of him. In fact, the *more* I expected, the faster he progressed. He was still protesting much of the time in therapy, but he was also making rapid progress when he worked.

Isaak continued to make great gains, but he had so much catching up to do that, at times, it seemed like it would never be over. Even though he was now using language, he was only chunking (using phrases taught to him in chunks) and not generating his own language. We began to teach him sentence structure for that—what parts of speech are and how they work together to form different sentences. We basically gave him grammar lessons generally taught in late grade school. Sometime around his fourth birthday, he began to generate his own language. It took another year or two of hard work to begin sounding like his typical peers, but it did happen. By seven, his language work was mainly pragmatic, teaching him to understand the subtle intricacies of language; but to the untrained ear, he sounded normal.

A similar progression happened with his other struggling areas of development like social skills and behavior. Skills needed to be broken down into small bits and taught to him with visual aids and rewards. After some time, the skills became a natural part of him. His ability to learn was just remarkable.

As of this writing, Isaak is almost eight years old. He has had a wonderful year in school. He is in a gifted multi-age class requiring minimal support. Mathematically, he can out-think most secondary students. Most people cannot pick him out of a crowd. His language can be a little pedantic and stilted at times. His social skills have blossomed beautifully, but he may seem aloof at times. His behavior has improved dramatically, even though he still shows the occasional frustration. We still work with him every day, teaching him to master advanced language and social skills, but we have high hopes for him. He will always *have* autism, but he is being taught the tools needed to function completely independently in society. Only those closest to him will need to know his struggles.

The term hyperlexia was coined in 1967 (Silberberg and Silberberg 1967) to describe children with unusually advanced reading skills that stood in contrast to language and social difficulties. Even though this term has existed for nearly 40 years, few parents and fewer professionals are aware of it. Parents of these children find themselves wandering aimlessly trying to find an explanation to their children's paradoxical personality. Most of these children have a pervasive developmental disorder (such as autism or Asperger Syndrome), but because their children appear so bright (as evidenced in early reading abilities), parents and professionals are confused, and the children often do not get the help they require in a timely manner.

Hyperlexia almost always coexists with an autism spectrum disorder, but it can often mask the autism because the child is so intelligent. How could the child have autism if he can read so young? I have heard parents say, "He doesn't talk, but he knows his letters and numbers" as if reciting the alphabet counts as a form of communication. It is confusing.

There are also a number of children who have been diagnosed with autism who may be showing early signs of being able to read. However, with so much effort on overcoming the autism symptoms, they miss a window of opportunity to teach them to read and thus be able to have that skill in their arsenal.

For young children, learning to read is not only an important skill in society, it is vital. This skill is invaluable for children struggling to learn the simplest facets of language and social expectations. Their ability to read opens up a world of opportunity.

Additionally, being equipped to modify a particular child's program to his specific interests and needs is essential. It's like a puzzle. Each child has his own picture, with unique pieces that fit together until the picture is complete. What a remarkable journey!

Chapter 2

The Walking Paradox

As a parent of a child with hyperlexia, I realized early on that my son was a walking paradox. In public, strangers often were in awe of his abilities. "How old is he? How did he learn to read so young? Did he do that math himself? How did he learn all that geography?" Even as they were astonished, I would think to myself, "That may be remarkable, but I can't carry on a conversation with him, he has no concept of friendship, and he has so many odd behaviors." At other times, when he was acting out or when his behavior was obviously different from other kids, I wanted to prod him to perform—to show off his remarkable skills—perhaps in the hope that it would hide his deficits.

Raising a child with hyperlexia is a constant struggle. You might think life would be easier if your child were simply gifted, or solely autistic, or merely learning disabled. At least then there might be a place in society where he could more easily conform. Instead, he might have a touch of giftedness, a dash of autism, and a hint of spiritedness; and he fits comfortably nowhere. You will probably have to forge a new trail. You will have to educate yourself so that you can educate those around you. All children are truly unique—there is no doubt about that—but your child with hyperlexia may be uncommonly unique.

Definitions
Hyperlexia

Hyperlexia is a complex disorder that, in most cases, coexists with another condition—a pervasive developmental disorder (such as autism or Asperger Syndrome) or a learning or language disability that is readily apparent.

Hyperlexia's trademark is an early and intense fascination with the written word. It is not merely early reading, however. A child may read unusually early, have some social oddities, and yet it may only mean that he is a bright, precocious child. Some children do prefer books to social contact, and that is not necessarily an indication of a disorder. Some children receive an autism spectrum diagnosis, and, although accurate, it does not offer enough information and direction to meet the child's unique needs. Some children never receive a diagnosis or direction, and parents are left to try to figure things out on their own.

The American Hyperlexia Association (AHA) has an extensive collection of information on the disorder. From their literature (AHA 2003) comes the following information.

Hyperlexia is a syndrome observed in children who have the following characteristics:

- a precocious ability to read words, far above what would be expected at their chronological age, or an intense fascination with letters or numbers
- significant difficulty in understanding verbal language
- abnormal social skills, difficulty in socializing and interacting appropriately with people.

In addition, some children with hyperlexia may exhibit the following characteristics:

- learn expressive language in a peculiar way—echo or memorize the sentence structure without understanding the meaning (echolalia), reverse pronouns
- rarely initiate conversations
- have an intense need to keep routines, difficulty with transitions, ritualistic behavior
- auditory, olfactory, and/or tactile sensitivity
- self-stimulatory behavior
- specific, unusual fears
- normal development until 18–24 months, then regression
- strong auditory and visual memory

- difficulty answering "wh–" questions, such as "what," "where," "who," and "why"
- think in concrete and literal terms, difficulty with abstract concepts
- listen selectively, appear to be deaf.

Dr. Darold A. Treffert, M.D. is an expert on savant and related syndromes. He defines hyperlexia as, "[A] combination of precocious reading skills accompanied by significant problems with learning and language, and impaired social skills" (Treffert 2002).

A research article published by the *Journal of Child Psychology and Psychiatry and Allied Disciplines* succinctly defined hyperlexia as, "the phenomenon of spontaneous and precocious mastery of single-word reading that has been of interest to clinicians and researchers since the beginning of the last century" (Grigorenko, Klin, and Volkmar 2003, p.1079).

Autism spectrum disorders often manifest themselves in ways similar to the symptoms of hyperlexia. One might wonder how hyperlexia relates to autism and if it is perhaps inextricably connected to autism. That is a matter of much debate right now. Hyperlexia is typically not a stand-alone diagnosis. This means that if you take your child to see a clinical psychologist or pediatric neurologist to address your concerns, chances are unlikely that you will receive the diagnosis of "hyperlexia." There are exceptions, and more children are actually being diagnosed as having hyperlexia, but more often than not, it will be a different primary diagnosis. If your child fits the criteria for autism, the likelihood is high that he will receive that diagnosis. If the diagnostician is a speech and language pathologist, the initial diagnosis may be Non-Verbal Language Disorder (NLD). Depending on your locale, the diagnosis may be Semantic Pragmatic Disorder (SPD). If the child is older and tested by an audiologist, diagnosis may be Central Auditory Processing Disorder (CAPD). Your educators may say it's a Learning Disability. Others will say your child is simply Gifted. There is a list of differing opinions which you may encounter.

How do you work through the confusion? Remember that you are the true expert on your child, and you have the power and knowledge to find the right diagnosis. Educate yourself and trust your instincts.

Autism

Most professionals use the *Diagnostic and Statistical Manual of Mental Disorders*, 4th edition or DSM-IV, produced by the American Psychiatric Association (1994) to make their diagnoses. The term Pervasive Developmental Disorder (PDD) is an umbrella term for all pervasive disorders which includes autism, Asperger Syndrome (AS), and Pervasive Developmental Disorder Not Otherwise Specified (PDD-NOS). You can find the actual criteria for each diagnosis in Appendix C of this book.

The three most common spectrum disorders—autism, Asperger Syndrome, and PDD-NOS—have a lot in common. Autism has three main characteristics: social impairment, communication impairment, and unusual behavior patterns. There is also a large possibility of a cognitive impairment. For the most part, a child is considered high-functioning (HFA) if there is no cognitive impairment. Asperger Syndrome is nearly identical to HFA, minus the early communication impairment, and there is no cognitive delay. PDD-NOS is a diagnosis that is being applied more frequently when the child doesn't quite fit either of the other diagnoses, but is still sufficiently impaired by many of the same symptoms.

It can be very misleading if you have a notion of what autism looks like, and you don't see that in your own child. Autism is a spectrum disorder, meaning that the severity of the symptoms varies widely. I like to think of it as a rainbow. All the colors are there, but the colors blend into each other and are sometimes more vibrant than others. Don't rule out autism if your child doesn't act anything like your nephew who has autism. Your nephew may have much brighter colors than your child.

Language and learning disabilities

There are a variety of language and learning disabilities that you may encounter in your search for an answer about your child. You can find a number of these terms in the Appendix C. You may hear Nonverbal Language Disorder or Semantic-Pragmatic Language Disorder or Central Auditory Processing Disorder or any one of a number of others. The overlap of these disorders is quite significant. Because many of these diagnoses are not listed in the DSM-IV specifically, diagnosticians may use their own personal criteria for making the diagnosis. Some of these disorders are diagnosed more frequently by speech and language pathologists, while others are more commonly heard in a psychologist's office. Do not feel that you have been misdiagnosed if your child receives a diagnosis that does not sound accurate to you. Many of these symptoms are identical, and most of the treatments are, as well. What's most important is that, if you are seeking a diagnosis, you acquire one with which you feel comfortable and will afford your child the best services.

Savant Syndrome

This is a rare condition where the child has a significant mental delay but also has abilities that stand in stark contrast to that disability. This is what was portrayed in the movie *Rainman* that many people still think of when they think of autism. Many savants also have autism, but only a small percentage of people with autism have savant capabilities. In most true savants, IQs range between 40 and 70, classifying them clinically as intellectually disabled. Nearly all savants have one thing in common—a photographic memory.

Giftedness

According to most professionals working with gifted children, there are two major categories in which gifted children demonstrate their ability. The first is emotional. They are the question askers. They are curious about their surroundings. They are astute to other people's emotions. They are aware of world problems and worry about them. They appear more mature than other children of their age and tend to gravitate to older children or adults. They are rule abiders. They like order.

The second area is intellectual. Gifted children have long attention spans. They can learn at a higher and faster rate than their peers. They are able to take a problem and develop the answer without going through the step-by-step process that other children need. They are detail-oriented. They are often visual learners. Some gifted children demonstrate talents from both areas; others demonstrate unusual ability in only one area or the other.

Where does hyperlexia fit?

As you read all these descriptions, you may find yourself confused or comforted. Perhaps both. Now you want to know where hyperlexia fits. It's obvious if you know anyone with hyperlexia that they are not mentally deficient. Many, if not all, have above-average IQs. Interestingly, the child with hyperlexia is often not so gifted in the emotional side. They do not appear inquisitive, struggling instead with the acquisition of sometimes the simplest language. Perhaps their language processing problems prevent them from asking questions. Perhaps they have the curiosity, but no way to fully express it. They are often plagued by a learning disorder or autism that clouds a sensitivity to the world around them that other emotionally gifted children may have. However, in most cases, they do excel in intellectual giftedness. They are intellectually keen. They learn concepts at a rapid rate if these are presented to them within their learning style. In fact, they seem to be able to learn almost anything if presented to them visually. Reading, math, geography, and astronomy are often subjects in which they far surpass their peers.

A child with hyperlexia can most certainly be called gifted. There is also more to the child with hyperlexia. What about the language delays, the social oddities, and the abnormal behavior patterns that most children with hyperlexia have? Most often, a child with hyperlexia also does have a form of pervasive developmental disorder, and in a fewer number of cases, a language or learning disorder.

Diagram of hyperlexia

In trying to understand the place of hyperlexia in our ever-diagnosing society, I needed a mental picture. Like my son, I am a visual learner. It seemed obvious to me that there are some children that are nothing more than early readers. They may have some oddities in their personality such as social aloofness, but for the most part they are simply precocious children who learn effortlessly. Then, there are those children who have a language disorder such as NLD or SPD or apraxia or countless others. They do not have any substantial visual abilities. There are also those with autism. They have marked impairments in language, social, and behavioral abilities with a range of severity. They are usually visual learners. Many learn the alphabet early and with relative ease, but that ability never transcends into true reading until much later. They are not obsessed with the symbols. Take those same children minus the significant language delay, with cognition intact, and those are the children with Asperger Syndrome.

Put all those symptoms together and there, in the middle, is hyperlexia (see Figure 2.1). Whether it is a child with a language disorder, autism, or Asperger Syndrome, the precociousness of their reading abilities sets them aside from their peers. These children in the middle are the ones who often make remarkable gains, since their hyperlexia could well be their greatest asset to make meaningful progress.

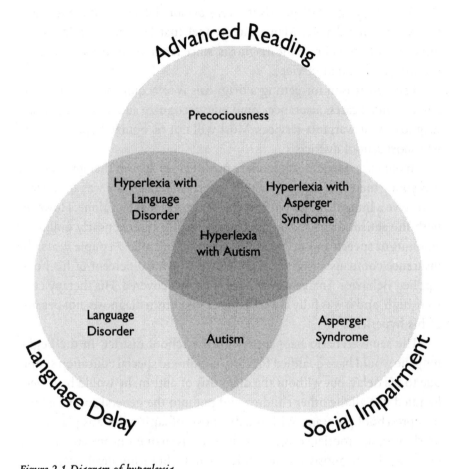

Figure 2.1 Diagram of hyperlexia

This is only an idea of where hyperlexia fits in the scheme of things. The disorder is highly unique, rarely understood, and it often leaves parents feeling confused and lost. The more you educate yourself, the more you can educate the people who work with your child, and, it is hoped, you will gain more insight into his exceptional persona.

To diagnose or not to diagnose? That is the question

Many parents, when presented with a large amount of confusing information, feel one strong emotion—overwhelmed. What is the difference between NLD and SPD and Asperger Syndrome? How are Asperger Syndrome and high-functioning autism different? Where does hyperlexia fit?

Deciding to get a diagnosis is a very personal decision and one that is met with much debate. Many parents feel that labeling a child can be limiting. Others embrace the diagnosis, since it opens doors to gain understanding and obtain services.

The best reason for getting a diagnosis is to acquire services for your child. In most cases, insurance companies recognize autism as a legitimate diagnosis that warrants services. Most will not recognize hyperlexia, nor will most school districts.

In our case, Isaak most certainly qualified for speech therapy when he was young merely by the fact that his speech was delayed. I was authorized to receive a limited amount of speech therapy on that fact alone. However, with the autism diagnosis, he was authorized to receive nearly unlimited amounts of speech and occupational therapy, and after a couple years, the insurance company instituted a benefit in which 80 percent of his home Applied Behavior Analysis (ABA) program was covered. His therapy costs were high, and it was fully covered due to his autism diagnosis, not because of his hyperlexia.

The same scenario happened with the school district. In the beginning, he would have qualified for early childhood special education simply due to his delay, but without the diagnosis of autism, he would have been handled like all the other children and put into the general special education preschool program. With the diagnosis of autism, he was placed in a much more appropriate class where he was given one-on-one attention. In our case, the diagnosis was not only accurate, but truly invaluable.

You may be able to get full services with the other diagnoses such as NLD or learning disabled. Perhaps a language disorder is all you need to get what you feel is necessary for your child. You will have to make that decision.

Another reason for getting a recognizable diagnosis is to help people begin to understand your child. Getting a diagnosis does not change who your child is. He has the same symptoms, the same weaknesses, and the same strengths as before the diagnosis. It is simply a way for other people—people that interact with your child—to have a snapshot view of the situation. Telling people your child has autism or a learning disability will not make them fully understand all the issues involved, but it is a starting place.

In our case, once armed with the recognizable diagnosis of autism, I was able to educate people more, not only about autism, but also to teach about hyperlexia. For Isaak, autism and hyperlexia go hand-in-hand, so I was able to use the autism as a springboard to lead into hyperlexia, which more accurately and specifically described him. Once he was getting the services he needed—speech and occupational therapy, a good school program—I was able to bring in literature and information on hyperlexia to help educators and professionals further understand his situation and how to help him.

Who should make the diagnosis? A specialized medical doctor is most often sought to evaluate a child with these symptoms. It was a pediatric neurologist, then a developmental pediatrician who specialized in such disorders, and finally the director of the autism department at the university who evaluated and diagnosed Isaak. It wasn't until after that third diagnosis that we fully accepted and actually embraced the autism diagnosis. Some parents choose to take their children to a psychiatrist or psychologist who has specific experience with autism and related learning disorders. Be it a developmental pediatrician, neurologist, psychiatrist, or clinical psychologist, these doctors should be your number one choice as a diagnostician. They not only have the education and experience to make the diagnosis but will also be recognized by insurance companies and school districts to get services.

Beware of other well-meaning people who yearn to make a diagnosis on your child. I've heard stories of school teachers, speech therapists, occupational therapists, and neighbor's friends trying to make a diagnosis. Seek out a qualified professional. Ask around to find one with true experience and someone you feel comfortable seeing.

Expect waiting lists to see the best professionals. You get what you wait for! However, if you feel time is of the essence (which it often is), put yourself on that waiting list, and then perhaps try to get a quick diagnosis from a less well-known professional without a waiting list. You can go ahead with services and, when your name comes up for that preferred professional, you can opt for another opinion and go from there. Having a second or even third opinion can be beneficial.

This can all be a daunting task, but keep your eyes fixed on what's best for your child and you will know what to do.

A personal note about labels

There has been some societal conflict over labeling children. There are those that say we are too quick to slap a label on a child who is struggling, and thus we compartmentalize the child. The label causes people to have preconceived notions about who that child is and of what he is capable. Some parents want a label so as to excuse their child's behavior or their own poor parenting skills. Perhaps they want special consideration for a child even if he doesn't necessarily need it. A label might get them that. These are all serious issues to consider. We need to be aware of such situations in society and work at getting accurate and beneficial diagnoses for children who really need them. We don't want to "water down" the diagnoses with children who do not qualify, thus taking away resources and understanding from the children who do qualify. Having said that, it is also important to be aware that an accurate diagnosis can be invaluable to a child who needs help.

I teach both of my children to see challenges and differences (I don't even like the terms disability or disorder) as nothing more than special circumstances. I don't think labels, in and of themselves, are bad: a label is nothing more than a word, and that word is nothing more than a description of a set of characteristics. We label people all the time in life. It's how people react to those labels that could be a problem. I've been open about differences so my children grow up without seeing those "words" with any stigma. Isaak was born with autism. And with hazel eyes, and being right-handed, and with an ability to read early. No big deal. I'm not afraid of the word autism. I just want to educate people, starting with my own children, that everyone has a different set of circumstances in life, and every person is equally valuable. Society should be better about that and see persons with disabilities (or differences) as being as valuable as people without. No stigma should accompany a word. No one should shy away from receiving an accurate diagnosis from a qualified professional. We can educate society on valuing *all* people—one family at a time.

When to be concerned

There are three red flags that may indicate a problem (see Figure 2.2). The first is a receptive language delay. Many children do talk later. You'll hear the story of someone's son who didn't talk until he was four and then started talking in sentences. I had a nephew like that and, in fact, when he started talking, it was in paragraphs. Usually, though, children have receptive language (what they understand) well before they have expressive language (what they speak). If your child seems to understand what's being said to him, if he follows simple commands, if he responds to his name, you probably have less to worry about.

The second red flag is a nonverbal language delay. Does your child use gestures to communicate? Does he point? Does he look at you when you speak to him? Children use gestures to communicate well before they can speak and then continue to use them to supplement their speech. Even as adults, we use body language, eye contact, and gestures throughout our communication. If your child isn't pointing out objects, bringing items to show you, doesn't seem to understand or care about baby games such as peek-a-boo and hide-and-seek, there may be something to be concerned about.

The third red flag is a loss of previously used language. If your child had language at one point, and then stopped using it, something is probably wrong. In some rare cases, a child may regress if they have gone through a traumatic event. If nothing disturbing has happened in your child's life like the loss of a parent or a medical emergency, and he has lost words or even an interest in speaking, get an evaluation. Most pediatricians know that if a child has lost language, he needs a thorough evaluation by a specialist. All kids will learn a word, forget it, then use it again later, but if the loss is significant and noticeable, there may be something more involved. I've heard of many children who were pointing out body parts, using simple phrases like "I want" and "I like" who, for no obvious reason, just stopped using those communicative gestures.

Your child is truly unique. On one hand, he is affected by delays and difficulties. On the other hand, he has these fantastic abilities. You may try to express your concern with friends and family, only to have them dismiss his delays because "he's so smart!" They may actually be right. Many children do speak later than their peers or have unique personalities. Some even read early. Listen to your parental instinct. It is there for a reason. If

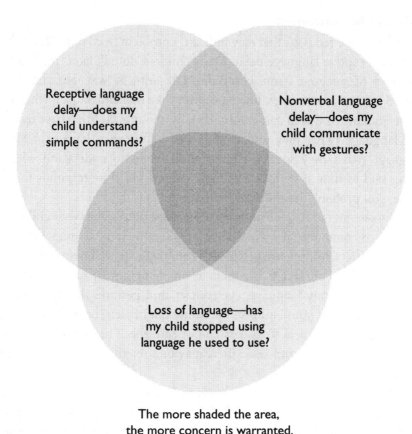

Receptive language delay—does my child understand simple commands?

Nonverbal language delay—does my child communicate with gestures?

Loss of language—has my child stopped using language he used to use?

The more shaded the area, the more concern is warranted.

Figure 2.2 Areas of concern

you have concerns, by all means, get an evaluation. If there is nothing clinically wrong, at least you will know. You can then search for other answers. If there is something more involved—something neurological—catching it earlier and addressing the needs sooner could mean a lifetime of difference for your child. Don't delay.

Stand-alone diagnosis?

Among the people I know, most children with hyperlexia are diagnosed with an autism spectrum disorder. Most have high-functioning autism or Asperger Syndrome. Some have been given hyperlexia as a secondary diagnosis. Some have a learning or language disorder and hyperlexia as a secondary disorder. A few have a stand-alone diagnosis of hyperlexia. What is interesting to me is that the general feeling about whether hyperlexia *should* be a stand-alone diagnosis is invariably: "Yes." Even though most of these children have a primary diagnosis of an autism spectrum disorder with hyperlexia either secondary or non-existent, most parents believe hyperlexia should also exist as a stand-alone diagnosis. Nevertheless, at this point in time, hyperlexia is not a self-contained diagnosis in most professional circles. Perhaps it should be. Perhaps someday it will be. But for the time being, further understanding and acceptance of the other issues is crucial.

Chapter 3

The Case for Teaching Reading

As a parent of a child with autism, one of the best pieces of advice I got from other veteran parents was, "The more, the earlier, the better." It was with that advice that I sought early and intense intervention. We began a home Applied Behavior Analysis (ABA) program shortly after he turned two and involved him in a variety of social activities.

Isaak's progress was quite fantastic from the very beginning. He was a fast learner, and it was a challenge for his professionals to keep up with him. However, I have no doubt that what accelerated his ability to learn was his keen intellect, as evidenced in his ability to read remarkably early. It was through this reading ability that we were able to teach him and open learning opportunities for him.

Create a hyperlexic?

Reading was natural for Isaak. I didn't sit down and teach him how to decode—only what the words meant. As I have met more families with autism and similar learning challenges, I have noted that many children with autism have an early ability to recognize symbols such as letters and numbers. Many of these children do not go on to obsess over them like a child with hyperlexia, nor does their early recognition of letters transcend into early reading. Perhaps it could.

Many people don't think to teach a toddler with obvious social and language difficulties how to read. But what if they did? What if that child was given another tool with which you could teach in all areas of difficulties? What a wonderful opportunity! People don't think to teach these struggling children to read because of that very reason—they are already struggling. They already have so many hurdles to overcome. Shouldn't we concentrate on his deficits and not try to introduce new concepts before he has even mastered the simplest ones yet? I submit that if you can teach your child to read, the child's deficits may reap the biggest rewards.

I do not contend that every young language impaired child will be able to learn to read early or easily. I do believe, however, that at least finding out if he *can* may be vitally important to his development. If you go on to find out that he is not responsive, that he is not learning the concepts easily, that your instincts are telling you it's too early or not the right manner to teach him, by all means, stop. If you find that your child is eager and willing and seems to pick up these concepts quickly, go with it! If you can, in a sense, create a child with hyperlexia, you will have more opportunities to teach him and find a way into his world.

Early brain development

At birth, the brain has billions of brain cells. The brain creates connections, or synapses, and breaks others away. No new neurons are formed after birth. In other words, the brain goes through a "pruning" process where it keeps the connections that are needed, and others are discarded. This makes the brain most effective. What it doesn't need or use, it gets rid of, and connections that are regularly primed and stimulated thrive (Hawley 2000).

Families and Work Institute held a conference in 1996 called "Brain Development in Young Children: New Frontiers for Research, Policy and Practice." They gathered professionals in the medical, educational, and psychiatric fields to research and discuss the developing brain. Their goal was to learn how that information could help children in the early years. I found some of their insights particularly interesting. One was that "human development hinges on the interplay between nature and nurture." They concluded that, although genetics plays a crucial part in a child's development, environmental factors are also "dramatic and specific." They point out that a young child's brain development can deteriorate or thrive depending on the level of loving nurture and stimulating environments. The second thing that caught my eye was that, "The human brain has a remarkable capacity to change, but timing is crucial." The committee determined that the brain is amazingly pliable in the early stages of development, and finding the right timing for stimulating the brain in particular areas can be critically important. It's possible to lose the window of opportunity. The committee then went on to make some recommendations to parents and public policy makers, but the one that stuck out most for me was, "Prevention is best, but when a child needs help, intervene quickly and intensively" (KidSource OnLine, Inc. 1998). It's a motto I have lived by for the years I have traveled this road with my son. I gave Isaak a solid early childhood upbringing, and as soon as I was aware there was a problem, I pursued early, intense intervention. It made all the difference in the world.

Making the case

There was a movement of teaching young children to read some years ago promoted by Glenn and Janet Doman, who run the Institutes for the Achievement of Human Potential. They specialized in brain-injured children, helping improve their intellectual, physical, and social abilities. A large part of their program is teaching young children to read, thus unlocking a variety of other methods with which to teach them. They wrote the book *How to Teach Your Baby to Read* (Doman and Doman 2002) in which they stated not only *could* young children learn to read, but they *should*. There was resistance and debate over this technique, stating that "forcing" a child to read before he is ready can be detrimental, and that flashing written text to a baby is not only unproductive, but possibly damaging. The Domans continued to teach and had remarkable success, especially with children with disabilities that others said would never learn.

Just a few years ago, the surge began again with a set of videos called *Your Baby Can Read!* inspired by Dr. Robert Titzer, a researcher in infant learning, and produced by Infant Learning Company (1997). Cable News Network (CNN) reported Dr. Titzer as stating, "There's a window of opportunity for learning language, and that window is thought to start closing by age four. Yet, we don't start teaching reading until age five or six, after the brain is mostly developed" (CNN Interactive 1998). Dr. Titzer was met with the same animosity that the Domans faced.

I have studied the works of both of these researchers and read many parent testimonials. I have found nothing but caring, loving people involved in this movement. These are parents who enjoy spending time with their children and who believe that exposing their children to new things, including the written word, is beneficial to the child. These are researchers and teachers who want children to succeed, who want the low literacy rate in the United States to improve, and who hope to help children with challenges become successful. As long as the child's overall well-being is the goal, teaching a young child to read can be a great experience.

Here are some more things to think about.

Pliable minds

I was perplexed by my child when he was little. How could he learn some things so rapidly, like reading and math, and yet struggle with other things that come so easily to most children, like talking? I finally came to accept that his brain worked differently. We needed to tap into the parts of his brain that worked well in order to help the other parts improve. We encouraged his aptitudes, presented him with materials and opportunities, and then used those skills to help his struggles. He was very young when he began reading, and his brain was like a soft piece of clay that was easily molded.

People might be hesitant to teach a child to read because he *is* so young. Perhaps it is the very time to teach it! The young child's mind is still developing. It is pliable. It is well-known that young children learn at a remarkably fast rate. Learning is a wonderful process that should be encouraged and cultivated, especially in the young child. If five or six is considered a good age to start teaching, why not four? Why not three? Why not teach as early as possible?

Prepare for later academics

Isaak began reading words at two, and by two-and-a-half he was reading well. His ability to decode words was never a problem. He could read almost anything within just a short time. Although he could comprehend the written word better than verbal, he could still read far above what he could comprehend. His comprehension slowly improved, but once it hit about a mid-2nd grade level, his ability to comprehend stalled. By about that level of reading, comprehension becomes more abstract. He was now expected to not only know the concrete information in the text, but to *infer*. Mysteries were popular, but Isaak could not grasp the concept of thinking ahead, of imagining what another person may be thinking or doing. He could only pull from the text what was there, in black and white. He began to struggle with reading, not in decoding, but in retrieving hidden information. He had been reading so long and I had already anticipated the problem, so we had been working rigorously on answering questions and making inferences from what he was reading. He had extra time to prepare.

If your child has autism or similar symptoms, it's possible that the academics in the early years may not be difficult, but as the years pass and reading and academics require more abstract thought, your child may begin to struggle. Concrete thought is not usually the breaking point for our children. They can much more easily learn the word *ball*, the noun, than they can *ball*, as in "having fun." The same can be said about academics in school. Up until about 2nd grade, children are *learning to read*; whereas, after then, they begin *reading to learn*. Instead of concentrating on decoding particular words, they have to start gleaning information from the text. "Dick saw Jane. Who did Dick see?" becomes "Dick saw Jane duck around the corner, glancing over her shoulder and breathing heavily. Who did Dick see and what was that person feeling?" If you have a visual learner who can learn to read early, you will have that much more time to practice reading for content, learning to answer questions, and making inferences and predictions from the text. You should then have a jumpstart on those skills so that when typical peers catch up in decoding abilities, your child may be ready to move with them onto more abstract academic skills.

More opportunities to communicate

Isaak was just under three when we moved to a new city where no one knew us. He was still struggling with daily living, and I had already learned how to use his reading to help him, so I didn't think about it much anymore. The first day we went to church, he was bouncing around and making lots of verbal noise, and I got out some paper and wrote, "Isaak needs to sit quietly during church. Isaak needs to whisper and talk quietly." The people around us saw this and saw how he read and then complied with the requests and were floored! What they didn't understand was that I could have *said*, "Isaak, sit down and be quiet, please" until I was blue in the face, but he would not have understood, nor obeyed.

Many children with autism are taught a secondary communication means such as PECS (Picture Exchange Communication System) or sign language. The goal of these methods is to help them learn language and ultimately improve their ability to communicate and comprehend the world. These secondary methods may also be beneficial for you to try with your child. Reading could be another, perhaps an even better one. If you can teach your child to read, he will have another means to communicate. It could aid in his ability to understand and use verbal language.

Reading, unlike sign language or PECS, is prominent in society. Imagine taking a *reading*, language-delayed child on a shopping excursion. The whole store is filled with words you can teach your child. Even when you're not pointing them out directly, he may still be looking and reading the signs. This will happen wherever he goes. If he can read, he will be inundated with opportunities to learn.

More visual cues

I used to follow Isaak out to the playground with a stack of index cards in my hand. I'd casually linger near him, and as I saw an opportunity for him to interact, I'd discreetly show him a card. "Do you want to play?" he'd read. The kids on the playground often didn't even notice. They just heard him talk and would respond to him. If he needed more prompting, I'd show him something else to say. It was a remarkable way to discreetly prompt him. Although verbal prompts are valuable, written prompts are even more powerful. You can be discreet and accurate in helping your child learn.

Special one-on-one time

I remember reading some of the writing of Temple Grandin, a famous adult with autism. She talked about her early years and said she is able to function as an adult because her mother never *let* her be autistic as a child. Her mother and a governess always engaged Grandin in some activity. She was constantly prodded out of her "little world."

One-on-one time is vitally important to every child. Children that are fostered in a loving, supportive, attentive home environment are better equipped to learn, even from an early age. This need for and benefit from individual attention seems to be even more important to the child with autism. More than just time, but structured, focused, concentrated efforts will give your child the best chance to progress. The time you spend with your child doing structured, meaningful tasks—like teaching him to read—will not be wasted. If leaving the teaching of reading to a teacher occupied with 24 other students is acceptable, how much more constructive might it be with undivided attention by someone who loves that child more than anything?

Reading promotes speech and language development

From the beginning, we used Isaak's reading skills in therapy as well as in his daily activities. There was a very obvious improvement in both his speech and language abilities due to that skill. It was clear he wasn't hearing all the sounds in our language, and what he *did* speak was almost incoherent. When he could read a sentence—see what phonemes and syllables made the words and where the words were separated—he could identify and subsequently make the sounds better. His speech improved, and people around him could understand him better. It wasn't long before the sounds he did make were fully age-appropriate.

Isaak's language abilities were slower to develop. Speech is merely the sounds, and that was easier to fix. Language, or grammar and usage, continued to be a big hurdle. Reading is still one of his greatest tools in that regard. We taught him grammar rules. We had him write a sentence he said and then go back and fix the errors. He read books and learned from them. There were countless ways for us to utilize this skill to help him in one of his weakest areas.

Because your child is a visual learner, being able to *see* our language is a huge asset. It can help him identify the sounds he is hearing and help him learn to produce those sounds. Instead of focusing his energies on understanding what the sounds *are*, he can see what they are and use those energies to figure out what the sounds *mean*.

Maintain attention

Like many children with autism, Isaak had little interest or patience with someone trying to teach him anything. He wanted to live in his little world and not be disturbed. The way into his world was through the written word, especially in those early years. When he was four years old, before he had really learned to play with other kids, we were walking one day in the school. There was a group of third graders out in the hallway doing multiplication flashcards. I walked by and Isaak was following me—at least I thought! I got to the door and turned around, only to find that he had sat down with this group of older kids to participate in their math activity. It was something visual in which he was interested and to which he responded. He would not have sat down to participate with those children if they had been out there talking socially, or discussing a story they read, or talking about rules, or an upcoming party. Something visual like multiplication flashcards were so compelling as to stop him dead in his tracks and got him participating in a group situation.

Your child may be so interested in the written word that you can use it to motivate him and keep his attention longer. I have heard other parents echo this sentiment—that they could try to say or teach something to their child, but it wasn't until they presented it in a written format that he not only became interested but actually began to understand.

Reading is a powerful tool, and if your child happens to be able to learn, no matter how young, it will be a great investment in his future.

Teaching guidelines

Of course each child is different, so the number one thing you need to remember is that you know your child best, and if something isn't working or doesn't seem right to you, follow your instincts. Create your own program with whatever information you glean from a variety of sources. This book is only one source.

Follow the child's lead

If your child is showing an interest in letters and numbers, try teaching him to read. Perhaps these are signs that he will respond to such an endeavor. However, reading should be fun and interesting and never considered work. If your child is showing a disinterest or disdain for this program, put it away and try it at a later time. If he seems to enjoy and gain benefit from it, try a little more. Experiment with the suggestions here and in your other resources to create a program designed for your child.

Never bore the child

You will have better success, and your child will be more interested, if you move quickly. Flash the words to your child quickly, so as not to bore him. Find new, unique ways to present the material. Don't keep laboring on a concept at which he has proven efficient. Make sure he knows it, but once you are confident he does, move on. Keep him engaged and moving quickly.

Prepare the child before

Before you begin this program, there are some simple prerequisite skills he should have. He should be able to sit and attend for at least a short period of time. It works best at a child-size table in a quiet area of the house, but if your child does better on the floor, then get down there with him. If you have never had your child sit and learn in a structured manner, use some basic techniques to teach him to attend to instruction. This might involve getting a bowl of his favorite treats and rewarding him with small bits along each step of the way—each time he sits when asked, each time his hands are quiet, each time he attends to instructions—and then add specific praise ("Good sitting!" "Good keeping hands quiet!").

Be fun and silly

This is so important. Keep things animated and fun. If you have seen the Teletubbies or the Wiggles, you know that young children respond well to silliness. Do crazy things if it will keep his attention better. Reading is fun! You are having special time with your child. Enjoy the time.

Teach useful words, not abstracts

Find words to introduce that are interesting to your child. Use your child's daily activities to find words to teach. Give him words that he will use in his day. Giving him meaningful, functional words will help him navigate a complex society.

Write legibly and with large print

Especially if you are working with a very young child. Your child may be perfectly able to learn to read, but young children cannot discern small print. Make the print as large as possible to rule out that problem. If you are adept at the computer, printing the words on index card paper is also a great choice.

Teach comprehension

The first part of the program in the next chapter is possibly different than other reading programs you have encountered. It does not start by teaching letters of the alphabet or sounds; it begins with teaching family names and other useful words. The first thing to do is to teach your child that words *mean* things. They are not just random sounds. They have meaning, and that meaning can be used to help your child. Once he grasps the concept of utility, then you can go on to instill a strong foundation in phonics. Many of the words you will teach will be taught as sight words, in a rapid teaching manner, with the goal of teaching your child to quickly identify a written word for its meaning. Whenever possible, couple the words you are teaching with concrete examples such as pictures.

Slowly enunciate

Make sure you couple the written words you present with verbal words. One of the goals is to teach your child language. Using clear language when working with him will help. Enunciate the sounds so that he can hear the differences in speech.

Always end on a good note

You want your child to enjoy the time you spend with him, you want him to enjoy the learning process, and you want him to look forward to sitting down with you again. Try to end each session when you are having a good time. If at any point he has a rough time, a frustration, or a compliance issue, you want to get through it and continue until he is having a good time again. You want the last thought in his head about the session to be a happy one.

What method?

The question then comes—what method should be used to teach reading? There are two major schools of thought in teaching reading to children—phonics and whole language. Phonics is the process by which a child learns the sounds of our language (over 40 phonemes in all) and then learns how to decode, or break down, a written word into those sounds in order to read it. This is where you hear, "Sound it out." Letter sounds are usually first taught, short and long vowel sounds, and blends of letters (bl, fr, ng), and digraphs (sh, th, ch), and vowel combinations (ai, ee, ie, oa, oi), and so forth. A child is taught to see a word, separate, or se-par-ate, it into those parts, and then put the sounds together to read and recognize the word.

The whole language philosophy goes about teaching reading differently. The school of thought here is that reading is learned in the same manner that talking is learned—through lots of exposure and trial and error. Children should be exposed to lots of reading opportunities with practical application and should be encouraged to experiment on their own. Reading by "sight" is often found in this system where a word is recognized by its shape and not by its phonemic breakdown. Many words in the English language, and particularly the most common words such as *the*, *one*, and *of*, do not follow phonemic rules. It's confusing for a child to be given a set of rules to follow and then to say, "But, forget about all those rules when you come across these words."

My son started recognizing sight words on his own around two. In the next month, he started sitting down with stacks and stacks of sight words—small and large words alike. By the time he was two-and-a-half he could read too many words to count. If he saw a word that he didn't know, he would either not read it at all, or simply mistake it for another word he knew that looked similar. Once we started an ABA program and he began responding and learning things, we were able to teach him better. At that point, I began slowing him down and making him look at the word more closely before guessing, and soon enough, natural phonics set in. He began to actively sound out new words. I never had to teach him long and short vowels or beginning and ending sounds. He already had a concrete understanding of what reading was. Once I was able to teach him to slow down and really look at what he was reading, then phonics took over. For my son, he started as a sight reader and slowly began to use both sight and phonics to decode.

My friend's son is different. She says:

At two, Jason was obsessed with letters. He would roam around the house reciting the alphabet. If someone else were to recite the alphabet or when we would go over it with my older son, Jason would stop dead in his tracks and get this faraway look in his eyes. He might even give a little grin. It was as though he were saying, "They're playing my song." Jason just turned three when I started teaching him phonics. When I was teaching my older son how to read using a phonics-based curriculum, I noticed Jason would stop whatever he was doing and pay attention as I went over the vowel and consonant sounds. The boy who had very little command of language would say things like, "Now it's time to do the vowels," echoing me. Since he took such an interest, I decided I would start teaching him phonics, thinking I would never see the day when he would string the sounds together to actually read. Within a couple of weeks he had down all the vowel sounds (short and long) and consonants. I began teaching him to string the sounds together to read simple three-letter words: pat, pit, pet, etc. After that, I introduced long vowel sound words: mate, gate, kite, etc. Once he mastered that, I started to introduce consonant blends, but quickly put that aside because he no longer needed it. He was reading with such fluidity for a beginning reader. He never slowly sounded out each letter in a word but would sometimes just stare at the word, evaluate it, and then blurt it out. Nine out of ten times he was right! When he did mispronounce a word, I would simply tell him, "long a" or "short e," whatever the case may have been. He would then correct himself immediately, pronouncing the word perfectly. By the time he was three-and-a-half he was reading late first grade, early second grade readers. On his fourth birthday, he was able to read his birthday cards. Taking him to the store was fun now because he read every sign and label in sight: "Mom, I want some Tropicana" instead of "I want some orange juice." Although reading at three is not unheard of, I found his fastidiousness and manner towards reading interesting for his age. He went from recognizing letters only to reading at about a second grade level in six months' time with really very little direction from me. I taught him the sounds and he just took off from there. The skill of reading is our torch through this tunnel of autism.

I am a strong advocate for phonics-based reading instruction. However, you need to take into account the unique situation in which you find yourself if you have a young child with challenges that you want to teach to read. For one, he is probably a visual learner—not auditory. He may not hear the sounds as easily as a typical child, and he may be able to identify words by sight fairly easily. In addition, you are going to want to teach him useful words from the beginning, for the goal is to give him more abilities and opportunities to communicate. In the end, combining these two approaches and adapting to the needs and strengths of your child will probably be your best chance for success.

The purpose of teaching your child to read is to help him improve his deficits. It is to have more avenues with which to help him become his best self. However, it is important to keep in mind that this is *his* journey. If early reading is not in the cards for him, recognize and accept that without hesitation. Help him realize his fullest potential, early reading or not.

Chapter 4

Teaching Babies to Read

Teaching your young child to read may seem like a daunting task. This program is designed to help you begin the process. It is a combined approach, intermingling sight reading with phonics. If you have decided your child is a candidate for this program, he is likely to be a visual learner and may have a natural sight reading ability. Teaching sight words early will give your child an increased ability to communicate, improve his deficits, and it will provide you with another venue for teaching life concepts. This program teaches phonics alongside sight lessons to ensure that he is getting a strong decoding foundation. Some of the first words you will teach your child will be functional words—words that perhaps a typical child might not learn to read for years. The primary focus is to learn to communicate, so keep that in mind when choosing what tasks to present to him.

I read a variety of books on teaching reading both to typical children and to children with special needs. Then I took my own personal experience and coupled it with the ideas of other parents who have traveled this road to come up with some guiding suggestions. Take what you feel is appropriate for your child. Change what you think you should. Eliminate ideas that don't match your child's needs. Every child is truly unique and will learn differently.

I recommend you try the curriculum as early as possible—when your child is young and receptive. If he doesn't seem ready or responsive, put it away for a while and try again later.

Preparation

You will need:

- index cards
- index card dividers
- an index card case
- a thick red or black pen (not too thick, but not as thin as a ball point pen)
- objects and pictures
- additional materials as presented.

Find a quiet place in your home; put a child-size table there and perhaps some shelves to hold materials. Teach your child that this place is for *table time* (or *working time* or *reading time*). Use the same term consistently. You may choose to not let this be a place for play outside of that time. Either way, your child should know that when he is called to that area, he is going to be in learning and attending mode.

When you begin, make the first few sessions short and fun, perhaps only five minutes. It is important to first establish that *table time* is fun. Once he is consistently enjoying your time together, you can increase the time spent working at the table, perhaps to 15 minutes. If you have a child with a long attention span, you may be able to do longer sessions, but go no longer than 30 minutes. If your child can only maintain attention for a few minutes, feel free to do several short sessions a day. As you and your child progress through the program, you will get a feel for how your child learns and what is most beneficial to him.

Here are some terms you may need to know while using this curriculum:

- *target word*: the current word you want your child to learn
- *mastered word*: a word that your child has learned and can now read consistently
- *target object*: the object that matches the target word you are teaching; this might be a real book if you are trying to teach the word *book*

- *blank distractor:* a blank index card that will be used as a distraction to the target word

- *word distractor:* an index card with a word written on it that your child does not yet know; this is used as a distraction to the target word

- *object distractor:* an object placed next to a target object as a distraction to the target word

- *receptive language:* what your child understands

- *expressive language:* what your child speaks.

The program is divided into sets. Each set has a different goal and focus. For each set of words, there will be five levels to work through before considering the set complete. The levels are *Match Word, Pointing, Match Object, Reading,* and *Generalization.*

Create each set by writing legibly or printing on the computer each word on its own index card. On the back of each card, make a little grid (see Figure 4.1). Sketch it out by hand or print a bunch on the computer and tape them to the back of each card.

As you go through the program, mark the level you are working on. In this example, the child has mastered Match Word (Level 1), Pointing (Level 2), and is now working on Match Object (or Level 3). The word can be considered fully mastered once all the boxes are checked.

	Teaching	Mastered
Match Word	✓	✓
Pointing	✓	✓
Match Object	✓	
Reading		
Generalization		

Figure 4.1 Example of a partially completed grid

Level One: Match word

In the first level, you need two identical word cards for each target word. Introduce the target words one word at a time. Do not introduce a subsequent word until you are sure your child fully understands the first target word. Once you get a feel for how your child learns, you can move at a comfortable pace.

Put the target word on the table, and then hand the identical match to your child. In this example, *book* is the target word. Say, "Match *book*." Your child should put the card in his hand on top of the identical card on the table, saying the word as he matches it. If he doesn't do it within five seconds, repeat the command, and this time take his hand and help him place the card on the top of the identical one on the table, saying, "Book." Once he places the card on top of its match on the table, say, "Good job! You matched *book*." Pick up the card and repeat the process until he can match the word on his own.

Once he can consistently match the target word when you put its match on the table, put a blank index card next to the target word on the table. This is a blank distractor. Ask him to "Match *book*" again. Give him five seconds, then help him, hand-over-hand, match and say the word, repeating the command and praising him when he makes the match. Do it again until he can do it consistently on his own. Move the cards around so that they are not always in the same position on the table—this will verify that he is paying attention to the target word and not the positioning of the cards.

Once he can match the target word with a blank distractor, put a word distractor on the table next to the target word. The word distractor should be a word your child does not know. Go through the same process, asking him to "Match *book*." Give him a chance to respond, assisting hand-over-hand if necessary, then offer reward and praise. Move the two cards around on the table and continue until you are sure he has learned to match the target word.

Once he can consistently match the target word with a distractor on the table, introduce a second target word. Go through the same process with the second target word without bringing back the first mastered word. Once he can match the second target word with a distractor, add the first mastered word he knows as the word distractor. If he continues to match the target word correctly, begin presenting the mastered words in random order with a variety of distractors. Mark *Mastered* for *Match Word* on the back of each card, and move on to Level Two: Pointing.

Level Two: Pointing

Level Two is Pointing. Your child will learn to identify the sounds you produce in saying the word as well as identify the written word in front of him. The process is similar to the Match Word process. In this example, put *book* on the table. Say, "Point to *book*." If he does not point to the card and say *book* within five seconds, say it again, and take his finger and hand-over-hand help him point to the target word, prompting him to say the word. Continue until he can consistently point and say the target word.

When he can point to the target word consistently, add the blank distractor. Move the cards around. Continue the process until he is consistently pointing and saying the target word.

Once he can identify the target word with a blank distractor, add a word distractor. Remember to move the cards around so that he is not memorizing the location of the target word. When he knows the first target word, put it aside and introduce the second target word.

Follow the same procedure with the second target word, using a blank distractor first, then a word distractor, and remember to move the location of the cards.

Finally, intermingle the target words with previously mastered words. Mark *Mastered* for *Pointing* on the back of each card when mastered, and move on to Level Three: Match Object.

Level Three: Match object

One of the main purposes of teaching reading is to help your child gain language, so the next logical step would be to teach him what the written word actually means. Don't rush if your child is struggling to learn the meaning of the target word. Keep at it. Don't introduce distractors or new target words too quickly if you think your child needs more practice. You can always back up if he seems to be getting confused.

Your child will match the written target word to a target object or picture—in other words, to a representation of what the word means. If the target word you are introducing is a noun, he can match the word to a real object or a picture of the object. If the target word is a verb, a picture of someone *doing* the action is sufficient. Make sure it is clear what the person is doing. *Falling*, for example, is a hard action word to get a picture of because it's difficult to know what the person is doing in stop action. *Swinging*, on the other hand, is an easy picture to obtain.

Follow the same process as in Match Word. Put the target object on the table. Hand the target word to your child. "Match *book*." If he doesn't respond after five seconds, say it again, and help him hand-over-hand. Reward and praise. Remember to have him *say* the word as he matches it. Continue until he can match the word consistently.

Once he can match the target word to the target object, add an object distractor. This is an object whose name your child does not know how to read. Prompt him to continue matching the target word to the target object upon command. When he can match it and say it consistently, introduce a second target word. Eventually,  intermingle the words with each other and with objects he does and does not know, and mark *Mastered* for *Match Object* on the back of each card. Move on to Level Four: Reading.

Level Four: Reading

The fourth level of the program is Reading. Follow the same procedure as in all previous levels. Continue to reintroduce previously mastered words, and change the placement on the table to make sure he is reading the target word consistently.

Sit facing each other. Show the target word to your child, and give him five seconds to read it. If he doesn't say it, you say the word, and then prompt him to say it once more. Put the card down. Bring it back up and repeat the process. Once he can read the first target word, introduce a second target word. After he can read them both sep-  arately, intermingle the two target words. When he can read both, begin the process again with a third word, and continue to intermingle the words. Do not mark *Mastered* on the back of the card until you are confident your child can read the word consistently during *Table Time*. Full mastery will not be considered complete until the target word passes through Level Five: Generalization.

Level Five: Generalization

Once your child is reading these target words consistently when presented to him in a teaching format, you'll need to make sure he has generalized the skill, meaning he can read the words just about anywhere he sees them in his environment. You can do this by getting out his regular books and pointing out the target words to see if he can recognize them. You can point out the words while you're shopping or on billboards or in the newspaper. Write them down in different styles of handwriting (not cursive, of course), big and small, on different paper and with different pens. A favorite may be to take his hand in yours and hand-over-hand have *him* write the word on a Magna Doodle, plain paper, or a blackboard. You can give him a highlighter and have him mark all the times he sees the target word in a magazine.

This is a vital step to take to make sure your child will be able to read the words in any format. Many children learn rapidly and seamlessly in a contrived environment such as therapy, but carrying over such skills into a natural setting may be more difficult. If you find your child is having such difficulties, try merging the learning environment with the real world environment as much as possible. Present more variety in your teaching situations. Try doing your teaching sessions in another part of the house. Use different word cards. Cut out words from magazines and paste them onto index cards. Do everything you can to help your child generalize what he is learning.

When your child can identify and read the target word in any environment, mark *Mastered* for *Generalization* on the back of the card. Your child now has another word in his language! Encourage him to use that word to communicate, using the ideas in this book if needed.

The Genelect Program

In naming this system for learning language, I have coined the term "Genelect," which, according to its Latin roots, means "born to read." Remember that you can apply many variations of this program—whatever is working for your child. Take the ideas presented here, and modify them to be most effective in *your* home.

Before you begin each set, you will need to prepare the target words, writing them on index cards and putting them in your card organizer. You can prepare a couple of sets ahead, but keep in mind that you will be adjusting the program to suit your child as you go along. You may want to wait and see how he is responding and what words he identifies with best. You want to provide him with a program that will help him be successful, continually adjusting as you go. Keep the number of target words in each set between 10 and 20. You don't want so many words that progress is frustratingly slow, but you also don't want so few that you don't have enough material to keep him engaged.

Write the target words in lower-case letters. If you have a target word that will be used as a first word in a sentence in one of your books, make a second card with that same target word beginning with a capital letter. Present it interchangeably with the lower-case target word so that your child learns that it is the same word. He will soon be able to differentiate the capital and lower-case letters simply through his word matching experiences in The Genelect Program.

Here are some symbols you will need to know in this chapter.

This symbol represents the target words in the set. Each set begins with a list of words in italics. These are examples of the target words you can use in that set. The set should be individualized to your child. Use words familiar to him; use these italicized words only as a guide and example.

This symbol represents a book you can make from the target words and sentences your child has learned. You can create it on the computer and print and staple it together. A simpler method is to cut and paste the pictures and write the sentences on construction paper. Do what appeals to your child's interests and what is easiest for you.

This is an activity for you to do with your child. Many of these activities can be used for a variety of target word sets. Feel free to interchange the activities with other sets and use whatever activity seems to fit you and your child best.

The first target words your child will learn will be familiar names and a few high-frequency words. The purpose of this is to provide your child with functional words to facilitate easier communication. In the beginning, you will not be introducing letters and sounds, although they will be introduced in time. Through this exercise your child will gain an understanding of how symbols represent sounds, and sounds create words, and words mean things. You want something concrete that your child can grasp in order to make language useful. Once he has a few words, you can create his first book. You can regularly make new books with the words he has recently learned. The books you make will be *real* for your child. There will be no teaching "The fat cat sat on a mat" until your child knows what a fat cat is and is familiar with the purpose of a mat.

Set One: Familiar names and high-frequency words

Mommy, Daddy, Jack, Rachel, I, see, love, am, for, this, is, want, look

Perhaps the most important words your child can learn in the beginning are the names to his family members. Isaak was two and could read and identify the meaning of many words, but he had never called us Mom or Dad. It wasn't until a year later that he first called out my husband's name when he needed help. It was a powerful experience for my husband that day, and I realized then that it was something I could have taught him the year before by using that reading skill.

For this set of target words, write the names of all your immediate family members on the index cards. Choose the name that you commonly use—if a sibling has a nickname that people use, write that nickname down. If you only have a couple members in the family, add teachers' names and the names of his speech therapist or ABA therapist if applicable. Add people's names as needed.

Take face shot photos of all the people whose names your child will learn. Make sure the pictures are clear and easy to identify.

In addition to the familiar names, include the words: I, see, love, am, for, this, is, want, and look. These words will not have pictures to match to in Level Three.

Familiar Names Book

I see Daddy; I love Mommy; I am Rachel; This is Jack; I want Rachel; This is for Daddy; Look, I see Jack

Once all the target words are learned, you can create the first sentences. Start by putting out all three mastered words in the sentence on the table and prompt your child to read them.

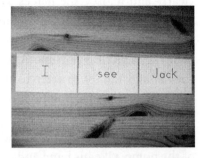

Once he can read the words in the sentence individually, create one card for each sentence. Go through the Level Three procedure and introduce matching the sentence to an actual picture.

Once he can match the sentence to a picture, you can create your first book—a pre-social script. Use pictures of the people you have introduced and the sentences he can read and make a book. You can take the book out of your learning sessions and make part of your daily activities. If you have a lot of people whose names you want your child to learn, you can make more than one book—maybe a family book and a friend book. You could also make a book of your child doing actions, using *This is for* _____ throughout the book. He could be giving a book to Daddy, a kiss to Mommy, a cup to a therapist, and so forth.

Nametags

The activity for this set is simple. All you need are a few nametags. Write clearly and legibly the names of the people whose names your child is learning. Have each person wear a nametag as often as possible. Ask your friends and family to refer to themselves by their name, pointing to their nametags when they do so. As your child interacts with people in and out of the home, take his hand and touch the nametag on each person, repeating the name.

Set Two: Facilitating words

time, go, kiss, drink, jump, stop, eat, sing, night-night, stand, up, stand up, sit, down, sit down, say

These target words will include those your child can use in daily activity. These are words that you can use to communicate with him. This could possibly give your child the first chance to make his needs known—a new level of language. If he has already been communicating his needs, you can further develop that ability.

When you begin to teach these facilitating words, it would be best if you could get a picture of your own child doing the action. If that is not possible, using clipart or pictures from a magazine or pictures of friends are all acceptable. It may be confusing to use a picture for the abstract words like "time" and "go." You may choose not to present it in picture form. The word will soon have meaning as you begin to use it in your daily activities.

Introduce these words in the same way you have introduced the others. Once he is reading the words consistently, present them in your daily activities. Some children may do just as well learning the words in daily activities at the same time that you are presenting them during your learning time. If you feel confident that your child can learn that way, by all means, go ahead.

A good way to make sure these words are gaining meaning in your child's vocabulary is to have them always ready to present in a situation. I made a set of index cards with these words and attached them with a metal ring. Isaak could read all the words, but he hadn't learned what they meant. If the opportunity arose, I'd pull out the cards, hand him the word to read, and prompt him to do the action. It not only taught him what the words meant, it was motivating for him to read and comply.

Facilitating Words Book

Time to sing; Sit down, Jack; Go night-night, Rachel; Time to eat; Go kiss Daddy

Your child needs words that help facilitate true communication. For this book, create new sentences just like you did with the first book. Put the words, on their own index cards, on the table and prompt your child to read them together. Once he can read the entire sentence, create the whole sentence on its own card, and have him  match it to a picture. Once the ability to read several sentences is mastered, create a new book with pictures, and add it to your now growing library.

Action Game

For this game you will need the action target words prepared beforehand (e.g., sit, eat, kiss). Sit in front of your child. Show a card and prompt him to pretend to do the action. Have fun with this! Liven it up by progressing quickly through the words or by acting out the word in a silly way. Have your child be the teacher and you the student. Have him show *you* the word to act out.

By now your child should understand that these written words have meanings and are functional. You have given him a strong foundation from which he can now be introduced to decoding that will be essential in his ability to become a fluent reader. Letters should not be taught in alphabetical order but rather in the order of the most-used letters in our written language. Some schools of thought even suggest you never even teach the letter names, only the letter sounds, because the sound is how he will encounter the letter in reading. Some letters have more than one particular sound, and in the future your child will also need to know the names of the letters, so I suggest you teach both the letter names and sounds at the same time.

Set Three: First letters

s, a, t, i, p, n, c, k, e, h, r, m, d, g, o, u, l, f, b, j, z, q, w, v, y, x

Prepare cards with both capital and lower-case letters so your child won't differentiate them as different letters. Teach both the name and the sound of each letter. When you show a card, say, "Big S and little s say /s/; Big A and little a say /a/." Prompt him to touch each letter as you say them, and have him say it. Don't worry about the exceptions at this point, just teach the sound that is most often associated with that letter (teach /k/ for C, for example). As your child begins reading better, the exceptions will be made clear and, if not, you can teach those exceptions when they come up. Teach the short vowel sounds for the vowels.

When your child masters a few letters, you can create a second set of index cards to go with the letter card. This set of cards will have a sentence, an image, and the letter. "This is Bb for ball," for example. Emphasize the letter and the sound. These cards will become the next book.

Teach the letters in the order listed above. The order represents the letters that are most used in our language. The first letters make good three- and four-letter words that can be used to create the first phonics words. You do not need to introduce nor have your child master all these letters before moving on to the next set of target words. Introduce a few letters to make sure he understands the concept and is on a good learning curve, and then move on. Continue to add letters to this set and keep working on them all.

 Alphabet Book

This is Mm for Mom. Say mmmmmm.

Create this book after your child knows approximately ten letters and sounds. You can use clipart for the pictures, or you can do a rough freehand drawing. Sit with your child and read the book together, prompting him to touch each word with his finger as he reads them. Add pages as your child masters more letters and sounds. The letters do not need to be in a particular order.

 Matching Bingo

There are many games you can create while teaching the letters and sounds. One well-known game is Bingo. You can create several boards in just a few minutes either drawing them or creating them on the computer. Some possible Bingo boards are:

- letter-to-letter
- letter-to-sound
- capital-to-lower-case
- beginning sounds (if your child is ready).

Set Four: First phonics words ă (CVC)

bat, cat, fat, hat, mat, pat, rat, sat, vat; bag, ban, bam, bad, bat

ban, can, Dan, fan, man, pan, ran, tan, van; mad, man, map, mat

Present words in this set for which your child knows the letter sounds. These first phonics words will be simple three-letter words (consonant–vowel–consonant or CVC) that can be sounded out. Introduce these in two mini-sets.

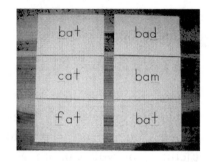

In the first set, change only the beginning letter of one word several times to make new words. These words will rhyme and are called word families. Prepare several word families and present them individually as families (all the -_at_ words together; all the -_an_ words together).

In the second set, take a word and change the last letter several times to make new words. Many children in the early stages of learning to read will glance at the beginning of a word and guess what the word is without sounding out the entire word. Teaching your child to look at the changes in the beginning _and_ end of a word will help him later as the words become more complex. Prepare several different word groups and present them individually (all the _ba-_ words together; all the _ma-_ words together).

When you make these cards, underline the changing letter in the set. For example, in the -_at_ family, underline the _b_ in _bat_ and _c_ in _cat_ and _s_ in _sat_ and so forth. This will help orient your child to the changing letter in the word.

Spend extra time on the first set of phonics words you make to ensure your child understands the concept—how to sound words out. There are lots of /ă/ words to choose from in this set; you can have as many words as your child needs. Once you move on to the other vowel words, you can have fewer words in each set if you feel he understands the concept sufficiently.

The sounding out process looks like this:

- say the sound of each letter slowly

- say each sound quicker
- say the sounds quickly and blended together (no break between sounds)
- say the sounds faster and faster with no breaks until the word is recognized.

Phonics Books

ăt book; ăn book; bă book; mă book

The Phonics Books are created from the pool of words your child has already mastered. If your child knows additional high-frequency words, use those in the books, too. It will give you a bigger variety of sentences—*The cat sat on the mat* or *The bad bat says bam*. If your child has a limited list of words he can read at this point, make the books very simple and concrete—*Cat. Mat. Cat sat.* You are still introducing your child to the utility of the words he is learning to read, so use any technique you feel is appropriate.

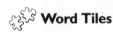

Word Tiles

The Word Tiles activity is great for kinesthetic learners—kids who like to use their hands. You can purchase or make these word tiles which are nothing more than small letter squares. Pulling from the word family target words, create a word, have him read it, and then change the first letter of the word to make a new word. Do the same for

the ending letter. As he improves his ability to read the words, step up the pace. Have him create words for you to read. Take the tiles around the house and find objects that match. For example, put c-a-t next to the family cat and have your child read it there. The most important thing, as always, is to have fun!

Set Five: Common high-frequency words

on, a, and, it, the, to, of, in, you, he, she, they, my, his, her

Increasing your child's repertoire of common high-frequency words will improve his ability to read practical sentences. Some of these target words may not have accompanying pictures—*the* and *to* may not have an appropriate picture. If your child has abstract thinking skills, you can use pictures for prepositions—a picture of a cat on a box for *on*, and a cat in a box for *in*, and so forth. If your child may have problems understanding abstract symbols for those words, teach the word without a picture, effectively skipping Level Three. The meaning of the target words will begin to make sense as he sees them in print and in context more often.

Prepositions Activity

By this time, your child should be able to read, or is at least working on learning, a set of prepositions. You may add more to your set to do this activity. Get a doll house or other play set your child is interested in. Play a game where you put the word in its position and prompt your child to read it. For example, put the word *on* on top of a  bed. "*On* the bed." Put the word *in* in a box. "*In* the box." Have your child do the same for you. Keep it as simple or make it as complicated as your child needs.

Set Six: Individual interest words

ear, mouth, eye, nose, foot, hand, bellybutton, head, TV, door, bed, chair, table, shoes, shirt, pants, cup, book, cheese, cereal, milk, candy, juice, goat, spider, horse, snake, dog

Identify five body parts, five objects, five food items, and five animals that are most interesting and useful to your child. These target words will become valuable as he learns what they mean. Use a picture for Level Three, most helpful being a picture of your child's own body part or favorite food item. For example, if you pick the word *chip* because your child loves Doritos, then get a picture of Doritos to teach the word *chip*. Get a picture of your own child's eye to teach that word. Get a picture of your own dog to teach *dog*. The opportunity to begin teaching your child real language is opening up now!

A Book about Me

I see my dog. This is my eye. I want a chip.

With the words your child has mastered, you can now make another personal book for him. This should be a book about him doing his favorite things. Use as many pictures as you can of your child's own body parts, playing with his own toys, eating the food, chasing the dog, and so forth. The words may be simple, but he will be learning what they mean in a personal manner.

Label the House Activity

If you haven't already done so, now is the time to begin redecorating your home with index cards. Start with the target words in this set. For body parts, draw a picture of a boy or girl on a piece of butcher paper, and label the body parts you are introducing. Put it up somewhere where your child will see it often. Print out pictures of the animals you are teaching and post them around the house with the words. Go through magazines and label the pictures you find and post them around the house. Anything you can think of! Once your child shows interest and is learning these target words, begin labeling objects around your house that you are not even working on. You might be surprised to find out how much your child is learning without direct intervention.

Set Seven: More phonics words ĕ, ĭ, ŏ, ŭ (CVC)

bet, get, jet, let, met, net, pet, set, vet, wet, yet; beg, bed, bell, Ben, bet

big, dig, fig, jig, rig, wig, zig; bib, bid, big, bin, bit, it

cot, dot, got, hot, jot, lot, not, pot; hob, hog, hop, hot

bun, dun, fun, gun, Hun, nun, pun, run, sun; rug, rum, run, rut

It's time to expand your child's phonics skills. Use the same procedure you did when you introduced the /ă/ words in Set Four. Choose a vowel sound and create words using that vowel, changing the beginning and ending letters to make new words. Underline the letter you are changing, and present them in mini-sets, emphasizing the letter change in each word. Use as many or as few words as you feel your child needs. Move on to the next set when he is sounding out many words confidently. Continue to present new words even as you move on to other sets.

 ### Phonics Books

Your child should have a good basis for beginning reading by both sight and phonics. Now is a good time to start purchasing and introducing beginning reader books. Go to any local learning store and ask for the early phonics readers. Scholastic, Inc. also has a great variety to choose from. If you have an older child, you may receive book order forms from the school. The phonics books are usually sold in small boxes as a group of books. Introduce one book at a time and make a big deal out of each success your child makes.

Phonics Games

This is also a good time to use beginning reader games such as My First LeapPad and LeapFrog Learn to Read Phonics Desk and other phonics-based games. LeapFrog Enterprises, Inc. has a great variety of phonics and other learning toys, many of them electronic, which will quite possibly hold your child's interest the best. Computer software may also come in handy at this point. The computer appeals to visual kids, so use that to your advantage! Interact with your child as he plays.

 Set Eight: Phonics vowel change (CVC)

pun, pin, pen, pan; put, pot, pet, pat; sit, set, sat; but, bit, bet, bat; bad, bed, bid, bud; mad, mud

Continue to build upon your child's phonics base. Do the same that you did in the previous phonics sets, but change the middle vowel sound as opposed to the beginning and ending consonant. Hearing the vowel sound can be difficult for a typical child, let alone one struggling with language. Be patient, and keep emphasizing the sounds.

Vowel Book

Similar to the style found in *Fox in Sox* by Dr. Seuss, create a book where each page has a set of these vowel change CVC words. Have the book start in a simple way with only one word set on the page, and then add some mastered high-frequency and other words to make it more challenging and fun to read. For example, one page may have "Bad. Bed. Bid. Bud." The next page, "This is a bad bed. Bid on it, Bud." Add pictures to accompany your story.

 Vowel Phonics Poster

Get a large piece of paper or poster board and make a phonics poster to display somewhere prominent in your house or in your child's learning area. Write the vowel sound with its phonetic symbol (short /a/ would be /ă/; long /a/ would be /ā/). Then write some examples of words that have that sound. Only write the short vowel sounds, and leave space to add the long vowel sounds in a later set.

Rachel's Phonics Poster

ă	ăt	hăd
	măt	măp
ĕ	ĕgg	pĕt
	bĕt	slĕd
ĭ	ĭgloo	fĭsh
	bĭt	pĭg
ŏ	ŏn	lŏck
	fŏx	stŏp
ŭ	ŭnder	sŭn
	mŭtt	bŭs

Whenever you have the chance, point out the poster to your child and go over the words and examples on it.

Set Nine: More high-frequency words

my, we, at, as, but, have, this, all, said, had, one, with, then, his, they, she, that, was, go

Add more high-frequency words. Choose target words that you think are most practical for your child. Also choose target words that you can use to make more individualized books. A thorough list of high-frequency words can be found at the end of this chapter.

Another Book about Me

This is me. I have a mom. She said she loves me.

These little books should be getting more interesting. With the words your child can now read, they can be individualized to his life. It will be fun for him to see his own picture and pictures of his favorite things on the pages, and it will be reinforcing for him to be able to read the story that goes with it. This will help the words become meaningful and, it is hoped, prompt him to start using them more.

Set Ten: Phonics long vowel (CVC-e)

mat, mate; bid, bide; can, cane; man, mane; pin, pine; kit, kite; cut, cute; not, note; tot, tote

Introduce the long vowel sounds using a CVC word, and add a silent-e to the end of the word to make a long-vowel word. Create index cards for both the CVC word and the CVC-e word. Show your child the CVC word first, have him read it, then show the CVC-e word, and prompt him to say the word

with the long vowel sound. Make as many word sets as you need to make sure your child understands the concept of changing the vowel sound when an *e* is added to the end.

Word Tiles: Long-Short Vowel Sounds

Get out those fun letter tiles that you used in Set Four. In this game, create a CVC word with the tiles, have your child read it, then add the *e* to the end, and have him read it again. If you want to spice the game up, do the Super-E game. Set out a CVC word that has a corresponding silent-e word. Prompt your child to read the CVC word. Then

bring in the "Super-E" (tra-la-laa!), flying through the air, coming to change the word. Fly that *e* tile in to the end of the word and prompt your child to read the new word. *Mat* becomes *mate*, for example. *Good work, Super-E!*

Set Eleven: Phonics blends

s-blends (str, spr, sm, scr, st, sp, sl, sc, sw, squ, sn, sk); l-blends (gl, sl, pl, bl, fl, cl); r-blends (pr, dr, br, fr, cr, gr, tr); tw, qu, gh, tch, ck, ng

This is a four-step process. First, introduce the phonics blends. Create index cards with the blends, and teach them. Second, create other cards that have target words that contain those blends. Choose target words with the blends at the *beginning* of the word, such as <u>cl</u>ue and <u>st</u>op, and keep the words simple with as few letters as possible. Third, when your child can read the blends more naturally, introduce ending blends such as ba<u>ck</u> and ba<u>sk</u>. Finally, teach the words that have both beginning and ending blends and are more complicated like <u>cl</u>o<u>ck</u> and <u>spr</u>i<u>ng</u>.

Nonsense Words

Get the letter tiles out again. Take turns making real words out of the tiles. Then, make silly, nonsense words. Make a list of words that are real words and another list of nonsense words. This decoding practice is important. It will help reinforce sounding out the whole word because your child will not be able to guess at them since they have no meaning.

Phonics Train

Choo-choo! Prepare index cards with the phonics blends written on a train car. Have another set of train cards with other combinations of letters that can join the blends to make words. Take a blends car and a letter combination car, make train sounds and be silly, and bring the cars of the train closer and closer. Make the sounds each time

you move the cars closer until they connect, then say the word. Make the train go around a pretend track. Have some fun! You can do this activity for any set of words you are working on.

Set Twelve: More long vowels

kee̱p, rece̱i̱ve, gri̱e̱ve, me̱a̱n, po̱ny, ke̱y, e̱ye̱, hi̱g̱h, fly̱, bu̱y̱, go̱a̱t, ro̱w̱, tho̱u̱g̱h

Prepare a variety of long-vowel words that are not silent-e words. Emphasize the vowel combinations (digraphs and diphthongs) by underlining them. You

may choose to introduce all of the same sounds together—all the long-e sounds like *keep* and *receive* and *grieve*, for example. See later in the chapter for a list of the phonemic conventions.

First Social "Reminder"

I will sit nice in circle time. I will keep my hands to myself. I will listen to the teacher.

This is going to be your first true social "reminder" book if you haven't created one already (see Chapter 6 for more information on reminder books). Pick out one skill that you are working on with your child. It could be anything from sitting during circle time, to using the potty, to standing in line. Pick something simple, yet persistent. Use the words your child knows.

Phonics Poster Amended

Add all the long vowel sounds to your phonics poster. Include both the mastered silent-e words and the vowel digraphs and diphthongs from this set. If your child is able, have *him* come up with the words to write on the poster. Make sure the poster is in a prominent place in your home so you can refer to it regularly.

Rachel's Phonics Poster

ă	ăt măt	hăd măp	ā	āte hāy	pāin māte
ĕ	ĕgg bĕt	pĕt slĕd	ē	sēat kēy	Pēte bēē
ĭ	ĭgloo bĭt	fĭsh pĭg	ī	pīe hīgh	flȳ bīte
ŏ	ŏn fŏx	lŏck stŏp	ō	cōat thōugh	fōē rōw
ŭ	ŭnder mŭtt	sŭn bŭs	ū	cūte sūe	mūle cūbe

At this point your child should have some good decoding skills. He should also be learning what these words mean, thus increasing his language abilities. You should have a feel for how your child learns, what he needs to learn, and how fast he learns. You can create and adapt the curriculum as you see fit. The more you use his reading skills in his daily living and learning activities, the more proficient he will get and the more useful the skill will be. The following are some more examples of phonics and high-frequency words on which you could focus.

Phonemic conventions

You may choose to teach these conventions in a certain order or randomly. You may want to teach them as they appear in the books your child is reading. Perhaps you want to spend more time on these as opposed to more time on the high-frequency words which follow. Since you are creating your own curriculum according your child's needs, you will have to adjust as you go along.

Sound	Example words	Sound	Example words
ă	c<u>a</u>t	ah	l<u>au</u>ndry, cl<u>aw</u>
ā	p<u>ai</u>n, h<u>ay</u>	oo	m<u>oo</u>n, fr<u>ui</u>t, bl<u>ew</u>, bl<u>ue</u>
ĕ	h<u>ea</u>d	oi	t<u>oy</u>, c<u>oi</u>n
ē	k<u>ee</u>p, rec<u>ei</u>ve, gr<u>ie</u>ve, m<u>ea</u>n, pony, k<u>ey</u>	ow	cl<u>ou</u>d, c<u>ow</u>
ĭ	k<u>i</u>t	silent	wra<u>p</u>, dum<u>b</u>, <u>k</u>nob, wa<u>l</u>k, <u>gh</u>ost
ī	<u>eye</u>, hi<u>gh</u>, fl<u>y</u>, p<u>ie</u>, b<u>uy</u>	controlled-r	p<u>oor</u>, b<u>eer</u>, b<u>ear</u>, b<u>ir</u>d, dinn<u>er</u>, p<u>ur</u>se
ŏ	c<u>o</u>t, th<u>ough</u>t	digraphs	ch, sh, th, wh, ck, gh
ō	g<u>oa</u>t, d<u>oe</u>, r<u>ow</u>, th<u>ough</u>	prefixes	un-, mis-, dis-
ŭ	c<u>u</u>t	suffixes	-ness, -less, -er, -est, -ed, -ing
ū	c<u>u</u>te	contractions	n't, 'd

Sight and high-frequency words

It's interesting to note that the 100 most common words we use make up about 50 percent of our language. The 25 most common words make up about one-third of our language. Learning these high-frequency words will help improve your child's ability to read fluently because they make up so much of our conversational language. These sight and high-frequency words need to be taught independently from phonics lessons. Most of these words do not follow standard phonics rules and need to be taught to be identified on sight. The following list was prepared by Fry, Kress, and Fountoukidis (2000), which updates the Dolch list that has been commonly used since its creation in 1936.

First hundred words

a	can	her	many	see	us
about	come	here	me	she	very
after	day	him	much	so	was
again	did	his	my	some	we
all	do	how	new	take	were
an	down	I	no	that	what
and	eat	if	not	the	when
any	for	in	of	their	which
are	from	is	old	them	who
as	get	it	on	then	will
at	give	just	one	there	with
be	go	know	or	they	work
been	good	like	other	this	would
before	had	little	our	three	you
boy	has	long	out	to	your
but	have	make	put	two	
by	he	man	said	up	

Second hundred words

also	color	home	must	red	think
am	could	house	name	right	too
another	dear	into	near	run	tree
away	each	kind	never	saw	under
back	ear	last	next	say	until
ball	end	leave	night	school	upon
because	far	left	only	seem	use
best	find	let	open	shall	want
better	first	live	over	should	way
big	five	look	own	soon	where
black	found	made	people	stand	while
book	four	may	play	such	white
both	friend	men	please	sure	why
box	girl	more	present	tell	wish
bring	got	morning	pretty	than	year
call	hand	most	ran	these	
came	high	mother	read	thing	

Third hundred words

along	didn't	food	keep	sat	through
always	does	full	letter	second	today
anything	dog	funny	longer	set	took
around	don't	gave	love	seven	town
ask	door	goes	might	show	try
ate	dress	green	money	sing	turn
bed	early	grow	myself	sister	walk
brown	eight	happy	now	sit	warm
buy	every	hard	o'clock	six	wash
car	eyes	hat	off	sleep	water
carry	face	head	once	small	woman
clean	fall	hear	order	start	write
close	fast	help	pair	stop	yellow
clothes	fat	hold	part	ten	yes
coat	fine	hope	ride	thank	yesterday
cold	fire	hot	round	third	
cut	fly	jump	same	those	

Chapter 5

Line of Attack

Even before I knew much about hyperlexia, and certainly before Isaak was diagnosed with autism, I had learned that he had a unique skill which I could utilize to teach him. When he started to read his first words, I got out a stack of index cards and labeled the house—everything from *couch* to *bath* to *door*. Cards sprung up everywhere, and as fast as I could put them up, Isaak would learn them. I knew it was only the beginning.

Your child may have an unusual ability—but not one that should be brushed aside or disregarded as a "splinter skill." It may seem like a useless skill when he can read words he doesn't understand, but that's where you come in as a parent. You can teach him what these words mean and how to use them.

Home

The home is definitely the first line of attack for your child. Your child will feel comfortable and secure there. You can manufacture learning opportunities that best fit your schedule. You can manipulate situations that will stretch your child in ways that can only be done in the comfort of your own home. You do not have to worry about someone asking questions or interrupting or shooting funny glances at what you may be doing. You do not have to worry about your child living up to all society's standards, but you can gently encourage him to move towards that direction—one step at a time.

Cultivating a loving, supportive environment can make all the difference. Sometimes, in the early days, it felt like all our outpourings of love and affection had little impact on our son. We would chase him, grab him, hug him, snuggle him, but in the beginning, little was returned. It was almost like hugging a rag doll. He wasn't one to push away, but he rarely returned the embrace. Over time he became more responsive. He began to return the affection, and soon enough, he was seeking it out. Even today, every time that he comes up to me and hugs me and tells me that he loves me on his own, I reflect on that. Those moments are treasured—every one of them.

Home is a place for the family. Spend time together. Have your child spend time alone with you and also time alone with your spouse or other adult family member. Have your children play games together. Teach your typical children how to respond and act around your child. Help them learn how to teach. There are times when your child will respond better to another child than to an adult. Exposing your child to a variety of people, all with different styles and personalities, can be helpful. Get together with grandparents and aunts and uncles; foster relationships with cousins. Having a large circle of familiar people from which to draw experiences can help your child expand his world.

Home is where you can generalize all that your child may be learning in his professional therapies. I was always involved in what Isaak was doing; I knew what they were working on in speech and occupational therapy and ABA and school. I asked to be trained or perform some of the therapy myself so I knew exactly what he was working on and what he was struggling with. With that information I adapted our home environment to mirror those targets. If he was working on naming animals, I would put pictures of animals around the house. I would take him to the zoo. I would introduce him to the pets in the neighborhood. I would look for any opportunity to work on that skill. Generalization may be a challenge for your child. He may be able to learn something in therapy, but taking it out and using it in the real world is something completely different. I felt that as long as I continued practicing at home what I knew Isaak was working on, he could better internalize that skill. It was a combination of a strong professional program and a loving, supportive home environment that assisted in Isaak's remarkable progress.

Outside therapies

Chances are that what you can offer your child at home, as invaluable as it is, may not be enough to help him make the progress you know he is capable of. There are a variety of therapies available. Some of these include speech and language therapy, occupational therapy, physical therapy, behavioral therapy, medical and bio-medical interventions (medication, diet, and vitamin therapy); the list goes on. There are a number of new advances as well and plenty of techniques from which to choose, some of which will be beneficial, and others will be inept. You will have to research and find what is in the best interest of your child.

Autism is a highlighted disorder in our current day, and there will be many people, some even respected professionals, that will profess to have the "miracle cure" or "autism breakthrough." Keep in mind in your research and investigation that anecdotal evidence does not a breakthrough make. As nice as a potential treatment sounds, frankly, they all do. We certainly went through the gauntlet in experimenting with many of these treatments in the first few years, many of them sounding quite promising. Most of them provided false hope and did little more than make our lives harder as we experimented. Research thoroughly; follow your instincts; try not to believe that if one family had a miraculous experience with a particular treatment, that it will work for your child. Your child is unique, and you will have to investigate thoroughly and experiment as you see fit.

Regardless of what therapies you choose to pursue, remember that your child has a unique learning style, and chances are that many therapists and professionals who work with him will be perplexed. You will have to educate them. You will have to make sure that they are using his skills to assist his learning. See that his hyperlexic tendencies are at the forefront of the teaching techniques.

I was lucky in that most of the professionals who have ever worked with Isaak recognized his abilities and were open to learning how to use them. Early on, the written prompts were used defensively. We wrote his schedule down so that he wouldn't have problems with transitioning from one activity to another. We wrote down words to make sure he understood expectations. We used game shows or other current interests as rewards for good work. As he grew older and progressed into more abstract thinking, we used his skills in a more proactive manner. We taught him social expectations by writing them down. He learned rules of conduct, rules of playground games, and rules of behavior. When he knew the rules to the situation he was in, he complied. He just had an unusual way of learning those rules. Instead of learning naturally from his environment, he had to be taught in a specific and strategic manner. He needed more than a loving home environment; he needed special assistance. I accepted and even embraced that reality—to his benefit.

School

Finding an appropriate placement for your child at school can be a challenge. School staff will probably be perplexed by your child. He may not fit into the autism mold, he may not fit into the learning disabled mold, he may not fit into the typical mold, and he may not fit into the gifted mold. Where he fits is probably into a small fraction of each. His educational placement will have to be just as unique as he is in order to give him the best opportunity to succeed.

An important thing to remember when you choose a placement is to choose one in which your child will be able to use his talents *and* be helped with his special needs. Both of those sides of him are equally important. If you neglect his gifted abilities, he may withdraw and struggle regardless of your other efforts. If you let him excel but do not address his difficulties, those difficulties will only worsen. Look for a classroom that will challenge your child. If the expectations are too simple, whether in regards to academics or special education, he may simply coast and learn that that's all he needs to do in life. Seek out a placement that will also allow him to shine in some areas. Let him feel good about his achievements and talents. Believe it or not, even young children with autism need to develop self-esteem! Seek out a place where he can feel confident and secure.

Accommodations may be needed in the classroom, depending on your child's specific needs. Perhaps you choose a regular education placement at his grade level. Chances are you will need some acceleration techniques in place to let him advance academically. You will also need to have an effective Individual Education Plan (IEP) in place to address his challenges.

Find teachers that obviously love your child and love his uniqueness. Have good communication with your teacher. Write notes back and forth. Be open and caring, yet be secure in your requests for what you know your child needs. Have regular meetings. In general, be an advocate for your child, but do so in a respectful and loving manner. Enjoying a good relationship with your child's teacher could make all the difference.

Other environments

You may find challenges dealing with your child no matter where you are. Sometimes going to the store or the park or church can be a major undertaking, especially in the early years. Feel confident that you can use the same techniques that your child has been learning at home and in therapy in the "real world." I used to write Isaak notes when he needed reminders, and he would be more likely to comply with that written prompt. I used rewards of letters or stars or points. If he was doing something he enjoyed, like playing at the park, and we needed to leave, I gave him written reminders and warnings. "5 minutes to leave." "1 minute to leave." "Time to go." All these simple prompts helped him understand expectations and navigate society. Learn your child's needs and what he responds to. Don't shy away from using these techniques outside of therapy and home.

Strategies
Communication

Learning to talk is something many of us take for granted. Most children learn with little or no direct intervention. As infants, they listen and respond, they eventually start making sounds and babbling, and soon they are making purposeful sounds and speaking their first words. Before you know it, you can't get them to keep quiet anymore! There are children, however, who do not acquire these basic skills on their own. Your child may be one. Whether your child is struggling with a language disorder or with autism or a related disorder, you can use his advanced visual skills to help him gain these vital communication skills. Here are some ideas on how to help your child progress.

Teach your child as if learning a second language

Children with hyperlexia seem to learn language as if it's their second language. Some have said that *reading* is their first language and *talking* is their second. Look at English as a Second Language (ESL) books to see how language and grammar are taught, and pattern your own teaching after that. ESL is taught in a very logical and simple manner—teaching rules, and exceptions to rules, and how to put together simple sentences, and how to create more complex sentences. Children with hyperlexia seem to learn language in the same manner, and they respond well to the same style of teaching.

Teach grammar

Pretend your child is much older and is learning these concepts as part of English class in the 3rd or 4th grade. Get workbooks from that grade range. Your child might enjoy doing worksheets, and you can find plenty teaching nouns, verbs, agreement, adjectives, adverbs, and so forth. Give him the rules of our language. It may seem backwards—teaching a child grammar rules before he can even speak well—and it is! But your child may learn many things backwards. Embrace that individuality.

Teach wh– questions

Your child may be able to learn how to answer the concrete wh– questions (what, where) easily, but the more abstract ones (when, why, how) will be more difficult. One way to do it is to teach him the rules again: What = Person or Thing; Where = Place; When = Time; Why = Reason; How = Method. Teach him what that means. Isaak had a hard time distinguishing between the wh– questions when he heard them. We'd ask, "What is a book?" and he might answer, "It's on the table." We wrote out a large variety of wh– questions and answers, and we color-coded them—all the *what* questions were blue, all the *where* questions were red, and so forth. We'd ask and show him the color-coded question and couple it with a color-coded written clue. When he could do that, we just used the color-coded wh– clue (for example, a blue index card with *what* written on it). After that, we dropped the written clue and just used the color. Then, no written prompt at all, but we'd enunciate very clearly. "WHERE is the ball?" "WHAT is a ball?" Eventually, he could hear the difference and could respond appropriately.

Focus on intraverbals

To be technical, an intraverbal is a verbal response under control of other verbal behavior. It is responding to someone's verbal solicitation. Intraverbals are really the basis to all our conversation. This is more than answering wh– questions. It is responding to what someone else says with something relevant. Intraverbals are gathered from three main sources: features, functions, and class. For example, the features of a horse: four legs, mane, long tail; the function of a horse: an animal you can ride or an animal farmers use; the class of a horse: an animal, usually a farm animal. If I ask *What is a horse?*, I'm going to get a different answer than if I ask *What is a horse for?* As you can see, there is so much to learn! Many children with hyperlexia struggle when they get to this level of learning. Concentrate on this area. Practice, practice, practice. Give your child the foundation for good conversational skills that should be right around the corner.

Practice bantering

Once your child gets to this point of basic conversation, it's going to take more practice to use those skills. Take turns picking something to have a conversation about. Teach your child how to respond to what you say with something relevant. See how many relevant banters you can get. Have him practice with you as well as with peers.

Play lots of games

Many children with hyperlexia love games, board games in particular. They like the structure and rules and often respond well to learning in that setting. You can actually purchase specific language board games from any one of a number of language learning companies. Ask your speech therapist for the latest catalog. You can also change any game you have into something specific to your child's needs. Change the cards in your child's favorite game to pictures of things on which he is working. Play memory games with picture cards about which you can have a conversation. Play Scrabble and talk about the words you make. Just get creative!

Create a dictionary

You can turn a three-ring binder into a dictionary or post new words on the walls of your house. Isaak had a binder for therapy time so that when he came across a new word, the therapist could grab the book and add the new word to it easily. The walls of his bedroom were also lined with "Word of the Day" worksheets. Once, when I said we needed to go run errands, and he said, "We're going to Aaron's house?" I got out a blank word sheet and added "errands" to the wall. He was so excited. When we came home, he happily announced to everyone that we had run our errands.

Social skills and self-help skills

Children with hyperlexia struggle with more than language, they have delayed social skills and often have physical delays that hinder their learning of self-help skills such as tying shoes and self-feeding. Even these difficulties can be helped by using your child's visual skills. Giving him concrete, systematic instruction in a manner he can comprehend will help him gain these skills.

Use written prompts

When we were potty training, we had trained Isaak to go if we took him, but he did not yet alert us independently. I made index cards that said, "I have to go potty." I placed them strategically throughout the house. When it was a scheduled time to take him, I'd lead him over to a nearby card, hand it to him, have him read, "I have to go potty," make a big deal about him saying it, and then take him. We did this over and over and over, until he was finally going over to a card on his own when he needed to go, saying it, and then going. Soon enough, it was ingrained and I didn't have to prompt him anymore. Trips to the mall were no longer a potty ordeal.

Written prompts can be used in almost any situation. When learning to dress, or tie shoes, or make the bed, you can use a list or a prompt for the difficult step. Right now we have signs in the bathroom that say, "Did you close the door?" and "Did you wash your hands?" and "Please turn off the light when you leave." Isaak thinks they're great and follows them every time. Well, almost every time. He *is* a boy.

Use social scripts

Social scripts take written prompts one step further. They can help your child learn to have a conversation. It can be specific—writing a script as if you are writing a play—or it can be impromptu. Avoid using the specific script unless you are fairly sure that the dialogue is stagnant. You don't want to teach your child what to say and what to respond to if it ends up being vastly different when the situation occurs. I used the create-a-script-as-you-go method more frequently. Isaak would engage with another child, and I could help him know what to say and how to say it at the moment. Perhaps it was a little card with "Do you want to play?" or a similar engaging phrase written on it, and I'd hand it to him, and he would ask the question or make the comment. Soon, no written or verbal prompt was needed, and we'd just nudge him and he'd respond.

It's important when using this technique to make sure you are encouraging appropriate nonverbal gestures from your child during the interaction. Don't have a script or a prompt written up on a board or a piece of paper facing away from the peer, but present the prompt in a way that will encourage appropriate body language, including distance from the peer, voice intonation and volume, and eye contact.

In Isaak's case, we would create specific peer situations in which we could use this technique. In the beginning, we would hand-pick the peers that would be patient and understanding but also verbal and engaging. When we'd script Isaak, we'd also prompt the peer how to respond so as to help Isaak be successful. Once Isaak had certain situations mastered, we would back off and let the conversation flow more naturally, and it invariably did. Soon, the skill was generalized and became part of Isaak's natural repertoire.

Learn how to develop reminder books

Reminder books will go a step further than social scripts. They teach your child about a particular social situation: what to expect, what is expected of him, and give him ideas on how to cope. These can be invaluable to the child with hyperlexia. You probably cannot fully understand until you have seen a one-year-old cradling a plastic letter as if it were a baby doll, or a toddler reading a book and stroking the words on the page, or a preschooler who chooses to read books rather than play with other children. Reading is often their world. Use it to your advantage. Your child will possibly understand the scripts you write better than any life's lesson you try to explain verbally. He will grasp the concept faster if you present it in this logical, written form. See Chapter 6 for more in-depth explanations and examples.

Encourage peer interaction

Set up play dates. Prepare activities that interest your child. Small group activities are also good. Isaak's speech therapist and ABA consultant have run a variety of social groups over the years in which he has been involved. These are great tools—not only to address his needs, but to pinpoint new ones. There is nothing like seeing that first budding friendship emerge.

Behavior

Not all children with hyperlexia or autism have behavior problems, but many do. Problems often stem from not being able to understand expectations nor being able to fully communicate. Your child may be frustrated and have no way to express it apart from acting out. Help your child gain the tools to not only understand expectations but also to adequately communicate his needs.

Be positive

There has been a shift in parenting and teaching over the past 20 years from a more strict do-it-because-I-said-so methodology to a more loving, positive manner in teaching. Parents and teachers are finding that children respond to positive incentives more than fear from punishment, and when they are positively rewarded, children are more likely to repeat the good choice. Praise cannot be lavished enough for good behavior. This is not to say that your child gets to reign supreme. It is just as vital to set up clear limits and follow through, but you can use positive parenting to make tremendous progress. A good rule of thumb is to provide three positive comments for every correction.

Use incentive programs

Taking positive parenting a step further, creating incentive programs for your child to promote good behavior is imperative. These might consist of sticker charts where your child earns a sticker for a certain behavior, and after a number of stickers, he earns a reward. It may be earning trading cards or marbles or money. For these types of programs, make sure the reward is attainable and clear to your child. He needs to feel validated and motivated to do well. Rewards are a wonderful tool. In the beginning, your child may behave well in order to gain the reward, but those good choices will eventually become part of who he is.

Write more reminder notes

Once again, reminder notes are priceless. You can teach appropriate behavior and expectations in a manner which your child will understand and follow. See Chapter 6 for various examples.

Offer choices

You might be amazed how much compliance you get when you make your child feel like he has some power over a situation. There is so much over which he has no power—he may not understand the language around him, he may not understand expectations, he is required to do things that no one is able to explain to him, and so on. Many behavioral issues may stem from not being able to communicate; he has little power in his life. One way to help a difficult situation is to give your child some of that power back by offering acceptable choices. If he doesn't want to come to circle time, "Do you want to sit on the red mat or the blue mat?" He doesn't want to eat dinner, "Do you want to eat the mashed potatoes or the meat?" He doesn't want to do a worksheet he was asked to do, "Do you want to use a pencil or a crayon?" Figure out what the purpose of the task is, and give him power to choose *other* ways to achieve the same goal.

Decide what is important

Pick your battles. Don't waste your energy or cause your child undue frustration if something is really not important. You will have to decide what is truly important and what is not. When you decide what *is* important, be clear and firm and stick to it. But some unimportant battles are just not worth the fight. As Isaak has gotten older and has learned to express his thoughts well, I have let him negotiate decisions. If he can give me good reasons and convince me that those reasons are sound, I will reverse a decision. I think those are good skills to learn. However, if I make a decision and I decide it stands, he accepts it.

Be consistent

Few things can add more anxiety to a child than not knowing if Behavior x is going to elicit Result x or Result y from a parent or teacher. Your child may be even more sensitive to such a situation. If one day you let him eat in the living room and the next you don't, you may be met with a large amount of resistance. If one day you let him walk in the grocery store because you're too tired to battle getting him in the cart, be prepared for a bigger battle the next time you try. Especially in the early years when your child has a harder time communicating, you will find that being consistent will improve his behavior tremendously.

Use visual stimuli

Videos can be more than entertainment; they can be used to teach valuable skills. A video can be stopped to discuss people's facial expressions and body language or what is happening in a scene. Help your child learn to make predictions about what might happen next. Point out people acting appropriately in difficult situations. Videos can also be used as a reinforcer. Give your child short video breaks in-between good work sessions. Perhaps your child can earn computer or video game minutes by good behavior and working hard.

Time-out

When used correctly, time-out can be an effective tool. It can interrupt an undesirable behavior and deter it from happening again. Have a special place in your house designated for the time-out. It's probably best if it's not the child's bedroom so he doesn't get confused or associate his bedroom with punishment. You want a quiet area, free from any pleasurable activities or stimulation. Boring is the key! If your child is still a toddler, you may decide to use a playpen to acquire isolation. Once he's a little older, a quiet corner works just as well. For a discipline tactic such as the time-out, there is no reason to express anger or even exasperation (even if you're feeling it!)

to the child. This is simply a removal from a situation and a deterrent for the undesirable behavior. Here are the steps I found to be most effective:

1. Have the place set aside and explain it to your child beforehand (as much as he can understand). Be clear to him what behaviors will result in a time-out. Write down these rules and post them in the time-out area. Even if your child doesn't seem to understand your verbal explanations, he may understand the written rules.

2. If your child is hitting or doing anything else destructive, no warning should be given. The first time he engages in that behavior, you walk him to the time-out area repeating, "If you hit, you go to time-out." If the behavior is something less destructive like yelling or spitting, one warning may be sufficient to give the child a chance to correct his own actions before the consequence. Do not give more than one warning for any behavior you have decided is worth a time-out.

3. Start the time. Use a timer that your child can read. The general rule is one minute for every year of the child's age. The current thought is that you should not start the time-out time until the child is quiet, and if he starts to protest after the time is started, that you should start the time over. Be strong. He will learn quickly that to get out of time-out and get back to having fun, he has to be quiet the entire time.

4. When your child's time-out is complete and he is calm, restate the rule, "If you hit, you go to time-out," have him repeat it if possible (using written prompts if needed), give him a hug and a kiss, and send him on his way.

You can find a large amount of information in the current literature and can form your own methodology. You should be able to research and experiment and find a system that works well for your family.

As an example, at one time, I designed our laundry room as the "Time-Out Room." I printed on a piece of paper, "Time-Out Room. Three minutes will start when you are quiet and sitting nicely. You will be sent to the Time-Out Room for the following reasons: whining, fighting, arguing, not listening [and then space to add more]." On another piece of paper, I printed at the top, "Think about your rules," and left the rest of the paper blank. On the rest of that paper I would write up the specific rule that the children would need to think about when something happened, for example, "I will not argue with Mom," or "I will not spit on the floor." I put a stool facing the door and taped these two pieces of paper on that door. I brought in the two kids (Isaak was five and Maggie was three). I explained that I wanted to be a better parent and help them improve (using language they understood), and I was starting a new Good Behavior Program. I showed them the Time-Out Room and explained how it would work. I made it clear what infractions would get them sent there and that they would be expected to sit quietly before I would start the time. If they complained, I would start the time over. All of this was explained beforehand. The first time it happened, I was able to simply lead the child, calmly, explaining that the such-and-such rule had been broken. The first couple times, especially for Isaak, it was new and exciting. He loved seeing the new rules go up. Eventually, the novelty wore off and it became a deterrent and a useful tool. They knew what was expected of them, and then all I had to say is, "Are you whining?" and they knew what that meant. I believe it was effective for Isaak because I turned it into something visual. He could remember the rules he was expected to abide by, and he understood exactly what he did to get himself there.

Loss of privileges

Although positive reinforcement and acknowledgement can be more effective than negative, there are times when a true deterrent needs to be used. For each child, this will be different. Analyze what is important to your child and design a system that takes that into account. I have used a variety of such systems over the years, each changing with Isaak's interests and responses. At one time, it was the warning of losing his end-of-day computer time; another time it was losing baseball or other trading cards. For some children, it will be the loss of a favorite toy or not getting to watch a favorite show or not go to an upcoming birthday party. This should really be one of the last lines of defenses and should only be threatened if you are willing to follow through. Only use this if a positive incentive program is not working.

Use his strengths

This may be one of the most overlooked techniques in helping your child overcome a variety of difficulties, including behavior. Because Isaak was so fluent in telling time, reading a calendar, and understanding money, we used those to improve his behavior from a young age. He was able to handle transitions better when he knew what time certain things were happening. We could put changes in our schedule on the calendar so he was prepared for them. We had an allowance program where he earned a small amount of money each day for good behavior and doing his chores. The timer has been absolutely priceless. We have used it in therapy, to let him know how much longer he had before a break. He earned break minutes by working hard. We used the timer for time-out, for time left in a desired activity before something new (to keep him from obsessing on something), for racing to do something. We just come up with any idea we can that will utilize the strengths he has.

Chapter 6

Learning Early Social Expectations

It is very important for children to learn and understand the social expectations around them. When they understand, they are better equipped to follow those expectations and, as such, learn and generalize those skills. For many children who have autism and hyperlexia, understanding those expectations can be more than a challenge: it may be impossible at their current cognitive level. While you should always strive for teaching that understanding, it may be necessary to simply teach the expectation required of them, especially if you are working with a very young and language-impaired child. He simply may not have the *ability* to understand the deeper meanings of the expectations you are teaching.

In one of our early meetings with Isaak's neurologist, I asked him what he thought Isaak's prognosis was. He told us, "The number one prognostic indicator is cognitive ability, which he obviously has. The second is social language, which is probably his biggest hurdle. Keep working on his social language, and his keen intellect will make up the difference. I have no doubt that if you can do this—improve his ability to have conversational and social language—he will do just fine."

We had always used his high cognitive skills to teach him. When we taught him his first communicative words through reading index cards, it was only the beginning. We found that taking advantage of his excellent reading skills, and then later his other emerging skills, has been one of the greatest therapies we could provide for him.

Because Isaak was so young and had little receptive or expressive language, we could not explain social situations to him to get him to learn social expectations. He just didn't have the cognitive ability in that regard. He was able, however, to obtain a basic understanding of expectations if they were presented to him in a concrete, written manner. He needed to know what rules to follow. His understanding of the reasons *behind* those rules came later as he matured developmentally.

In order to take advantage of this opportunity to teach, I began writing small "reminder" books for Isaak to read. The purpose was to explain a social situation in simple, concrete terms, give him the behavior expectations and words to use, and reward him for abiding by those expectations.

One of the earliest ones was "Isaak's Book." He had just started to read, and I wanted to show him how the words he could read had real meaning. It was simple and descriptive. There was no social skill to learn other than learning that reading had meaning. "Isaak goes bye-bye" and "Maggie goes night-night" and "Isaak plays ball" were all accompanied by pictures of what was being described.

"Isaak goes to church" was written when he was having a hard time sitting quietly during church. He had a loud voice and would make noises throughout the whole service. This book went like this:

On Sunday, I go to church with Mommy, Daddy, and Maggie.

Usually at church, people are quiet.

I can sit on the bench. I will whisper and talk quietly [*telling him the same thing in several different ways helped make sure he understood*].

I can read a book or color or write on paper [*giving him several options from which to choose*].

I will wait for the bread and water quietly [*restating the expectation*].

After the bread and water, I get a drink [*a sippy cup drink was the reward for him at the time*].

I will continue to sit quietly and whisper. After, I go to nursery!

Yea! I do a great job at church and Mommy and Daddy are so proud of me!

I read the book to him once or twice, and then he began to read it to himself. He thought the book was great! I brought it to church, and when he would get too loud, I would pull out the book, and he would read it quietly to himself. He would then comply. If he forgot and began to get loud again, I would point to the particular page that was appropriate, and he would quiet down again. Soon enough, he didn't need the book at all, and church became an enjoyable experience.

I read *Hannah's Hope* (Kovach 1999) written by Renee Montero Kovach who had a child with hyperlexia. Kovach used a similar technique, but she would alternate third person telling the story and a first person sentence that was repeated throughout the story that presented the "rule" or the expected result. I thought this was a great idea and decided to give it a try. I would take pictures of the situation being discussed in the book and use real pictures to illustrate the books, and if I couldn't, I used clipart. I kept the numbers of words on a page to a minimum to make sure Isaak understood the language, and as he got older and his language abilities became more advanced, I was able to have more detailed instructions and reasoning. I created three different kinds of these books: the Reminder Book, the Situation Book, and the Incentive Chart. Be advised that some of these are explicit. Sometimes we have to forgo our own social quirks in order to help our children get over theirs!

Reminder Book

The Reminder Book is a book about one particular expectation. It presents the expectation and gives your child the appropriate words or gestures he needs to become socially compatible with his peers. This is where I used Kovach's model.

It took some practice to find the right tone and language that worked best for Isaak. He responded to simple language that was repetitive and upbeat. He needed to know exactly what was expected of him, and when he saw it in written form, it became concrete in his mind, and he was able to comply. Having an expectation written down for him alleviated the anxiety of not understanding what was happening nor what was expected of him. There was comfort to be found for him in these books.

I found that once he read and remembered the expectation for each story, the behaviors disappeared almost immediately. Once he knew the book well, if he needed it, I could just remind him, "What does your book say about *Using Words?*" and he would repeat the first person statement to me, "I will remember to use my words" and usually comply.

Here are some examples of reminder books.

Using Words

When Isaak is at school, sometimes he gets frustrated or angry. Sometimes he can't finish a puzzle. Sometimes he has to do something out of order. Sometimes he can't play with something he wants to play with. That's OK!

I will remember to use my words.

When Isaak gets frustrated, he can just tell the teacher by using his words why he is upset. She will help him work things out.

I will remember to use my words.

Isaak is getting bigger. He is almost 5 years old! He does not need to cry when he is angry. He can just use his words. When he remembers to use his words, he will get to play with all sorts of fun things—like math and reading and the United States puzzle. He will have lots of friends and will have a good time at school.

I will remember to use my words.

When Isaak remembers to use his words, he shows he is a big boy. His teacher and his mom and dad are so very proud of him.

Hands to Self

Sometimes Isaak gets very excited. That is good! He wants to play with his friends or he likes a toy. Isaak should be gentle and remember to keep his hands to himself.

I will keep my hands to myself.

Isaak is a very happy boy. He wants to be liked by the other kids. The other kids want to play with Isaak when he is gentle. He can do it!

I will keep my hands to myself.

Isaak is doing so well in school! He is making new friends, and he is playing with lots of fun things. When he keeps his hands to himself, everyone is happy. His teacher and Mommy and Daddy are so very happy and proud of him.

I will keep my hands to myself.

Using the Potty

Isaak is getting to be a big boy. He does not wear a diaper anymore.

He goes wee-wee and poo-poo in the potty now.

When I need to go wee-wee or poo-poo I remember to say, "I have to go potty."

Just like Joshua and Bear, when he feels wee-wee or poo-poo coming out, he says, "I have to go potty" and goes to the bathroom. He sits on the potty!

When I need to go wee-wee or poo-poo I remember to say, "I have to go potty."

He waits for the wee-wee and poo-poo to come out. Then, he uses toilet paper to wipe himself. He pulls up his undies and pants. What a big boy!

When I need to go wee-wee or poo-poo I remember to say, "I have to go potty."

Isaak washes his hands. Boy, does he feel better!

When I need to go wee-wee or poo-poo I remember to say, "I have to go potty."

Isaak remembers to keep his undies clean and dry. No wee-wee or poo-poo in his undies!

When I need to go wee-wee or poo-poo I remember to say, "I have to go potty."

If Isaak keeps his undies dry all day and goes wee-wee and poo-poo in the potty all day, and at 7:00 at night, he gets a letter sticker. He is so happy when he gets a sticker. Great potty day, Isaak!

When I need to go wee-wee or poo-poo I remember to say, "I have to go potty."

My Social Skills

Isaak is learning to talk better and ask lots of great questions. It's fun to talk. He can ask his friends all sorts of questions.

I will remember my talking rules.

Isaak can ask another kid how old he is. He should not ask adults how old they are. That is rude! Isaak should not ask a woman if she is having a baby. He should never tell her she has a fat tummy. That might make her feel sad. A woman likes to hear that she is beautiful!

I will remember my talking rules.

Isaak can think of lots of good things to say to his teachers and other adults. He can say she looks pretty. He can say she is nice. He can say that she is his friend. He should not say that he loves her. Love is for Mommy and Daddy. He probably shouldn't kiss her. Kisses are only for Mommy and Daddy.

I will remember my talking rules.

Mommy and Daddy and all of Isaak's teachers are so proud of him. He is talking so good! He is learning to have conversations and learn things about his friends and his teachers. That is wonderful. If he follows these simple rules, he will make more friends, and his teachers will love to be around him.

I will remember my talking rules.

Isaak's Xbox Book

Isaak loves to play Xbox. It is his favorite game. He likes to play Amped and Fusion Frenzy and Project Gotham Racing.

If I follow all my rules, I get to play Xbox.

Isaak gets to play Xbox when he follows his rules. He needs to stay dry at night, follow the rules at school, and work hard during the day. He also needs to play nice with Maggie and be happy during the day. Then, he gets the reward of playing Xbox!

Sometimes Mommy or Daddy tell Isaak it's time to turn off the Xbox. But he still wants to play! Isaak can remember that he can play another time.

I will be happy to turn off Xbox when Mommy or Daddy says it's time.

Sometimes Mommy and Daddy play with Isaak when he plays Xbox. Sometimes they don't. That's OK! Isaak can still have fun if he has to play by himself.

It's OK if I have to play Xbox by myself.

If Mommy or Daddy tell Isaak he can't play Xbox, if there isn't time or he hasn't followed the rules, then Isaak does not need to cry. He can talk to Mommy or Daddy. He can remember that he can play another time!

It is OK if I can't play Xbox sometimes. I will remember I can play another time.

Isaak is getting to be such a big boy. Mommy and Daddy like to play with Isaak and are so proud of him!

I Make Good Choices!

Sometimes Isaak sees things that are cool that he'd like to have. Maybe it's something with numbers. Maybe it's a cool game. Maybe it's something he wants to eat.

I only take things that belong to me.

If Isaak sees something interesting, this is what he can do:

1. He can ask an adult to find out whose cool thing it is.
2. He can ask that person if he can look at it or play with it.
3. If that person says yes, he can play with it for a few minutes, then he will give it back.
4. If that person says no, he will give it back right then.
5. He can remember what the cool thing is and tell Mommy later about it.

I only take things that belong to me.

Isaak will remember to think before he acts. He will think about how his actions will affect other people. If he takes something that is not his, he could make someone sad or angry. If he takes something that is not his, he could put someone in danger. He needs to remember these things before he acts.

I only take things that belong to me.

Isaak is learning to respect other people's property. That means that he thinks about his actions before he does anything. He thinks about how other people feel and makes his choices thinking about them. He is choosing the right! And when he chooses the right, he feels good, and other people are proud of him.

Situation Book

The second type of book I created was the Situation Book. It is a book that encompasses all the expectations in a particular social situation. With some of these books, I could continue to add expectations to the book as different issues emerged. Isaak loved to see a new expectation added to a book.

I Go Swimming

My name is Isaak. I like to swim. On most Fridays, I get to go swimming with Sara! We start at 2:00.

When I get to the pool, I go in a room and get dressed. Sometimes I have to go potty. I take off my old clothes and put on my swimming suit and swimming shoes. Then, I am ready to go swimming!

I take a quick shower, and then I walk to the swimming pool with Mommy and Sara.

I listen to Sara so I can learn to swim. She tells me what to do.

1. Start at the wall
2. Jump in
3. Turn back to the wall
4. Put my face in
5. Blow bubbles
6. Reach out and pull the water with my arms
7. Kick my feet
8. Reach the wall. Hooray!

Sometimes we play games like Ring Around the Rosie and Humpty Dumpty. We sing songs.

I remember to put my face in and blow bubbles. I remember to kick my feet and reach with my arms. Soon I will be swimming!

At 3:00 it's time to say good-bye. We sing our good-bye song and then get out of the water. We say good-bye to Sara. Until next Friday!

I go shower and take my wet clothes off. Mommy helps me get dressed and we go to the blue car to go home. Hooray! Swimming is fun!

Reminder Book about School

I get to go to school with my friends. School is fun. My teachers are nice. I say "Hi" to all my friends and my teacher when I arrive. I put my coat away and find something to play with.

Use a quiet voice.

I remember to use my inside voice. I remember to talk quietly and whisper when I am inside.

Listen to the teacher.

I listen to the teacher at all times. I obey and do what I'm told. If I don't understand, she can write it down for me or give me a checklist or a schedule to help me.

Sit during circle time.

I will remember to sit good during circle time. I will sit on my bottom and keep my hands still. I will raise my hand and wait to be called on to answer. My teacher likes to see me raise my hand. Then she knows I have something to say and she can call on me to hear it.

Take small bites.

I am learning to eat lots of new foods. That is good for my body. It will make me strong. I will take small bites when I eat. I do not want to choke! So, I will remember to take a small bite, chew, and swallow. Small bite, chew, swallow.

Look in the eye.

I remember to look in my friend's or teacher's eyes when I talk to them. They like to see my eyes. It helps them feel comfortable talking to me.

Sit at the table for lunch.

I will sit with the kids during lunch. If I don't want to eat, I need to sit at the table anyway. When the teacher says it's OK, I can get up and go play.

Play nice and keep hands to myself.

I play nice with my friends. I use a nice voice. I share my toys. I keep my hands to myself. It makes my friends happy!

Be happy!

I will not cry or scream or say "No" to my friends or teacher. I will use my words and say what I want. I will show my happy face.

Play with friends.

I have lots of friends at school and home. They like to play with me. I will remember to ask them to play, and I will play with them when they ask me. Playing with friends is fun!

I really like school a lot. I want to be there. When I remember these things, I get to go to school and play with all the wonderful things and see all my friends. School is very fun for me! My teacher and Mommy and Daddy are so happy, and I can play and learn at school.

Another Reminder Book about School

Isaak is in kindergarten! He is making lots of new friends and learning lots of great things. He loves school. Here are some things to remember that will help him continue to have a wonderful year.

Resolve conflicts

Sometimes I have a conflict with a friend in class or on the playground. I can do lots of things to resolve the conflict. I can try to talk calmly to the other kid. I can talk to a teacher. If I feel angry, I can stop and count to ten or sing a song. I can always just walk away. I should never hit, kick, bite, or pull hair. I don't want to hurt my friends. It's so much more fun to get along! If I remember to resolve my conflict calmly, my parents and my teachers will be very proud of me.

Waiting in line

There are lots of times at school that I have to wait in line. Sometimes it's to go to recess. Sometimes it's to go to art class or music class. Sometimes it's to show my work to my teacher. I need to remember to wait patiently and quietly for my turn. I will keep my hands to myself. I will stay in line the whole time and not wander away to do something else. If I do these things, I will get to do the next thing quicker, and I will have a great time!

Taking tests

At school, sometimes I have to take tests. My reading tests are very important. They help me learn things. When I read my book, I will remember to read slowly and pay attention to everything the book says. Then, when I take the test, I will read each question carefully, think of the answer, then select the answer on the computer. I will remember to go slowly and think about my answers well. If I do that, I will do better on the test; maybe even get a 100 percent! It feels good to do well.

Eating lunch

I love lunchtime! Some days I get to eat hot lunch. When I get hot lunch, I need to eat as much as I can so my tummy will be full. I don't want to be hungry later. Many days, I take cold lunch. When I eat cold lunch, I can eat all the lunch I want at one time and save all my garbage in my lunchbox. Then, when I'm all done, I can throw away all my garbage together. That way, I only have to go to the garbage one time.

Paying attention

Sometimes I have to listen with lots of other kids to the teacher or other kids. I should pay attention and listen to whoever is speaking because it might be important for me! Sometimes, it's not something I understand or am interested in, but I still need to look at the speaker and try to listen. This is polite. If I have something to say, I will raise my hand and wait to be called on. When it's my turn to stand up and talk, I will speak clearly and slowly and look in people's eyes. Then, they will be interested in what I have to say!

Staying on task

During seatwork, I will concentrate on my work. I will try not to get distracted and think of other things. I want to get done with my work so I can have free time and recess! I will remember what I should be working on and get it done right away. I will be accurate and neat in my work so my teacher can see my good work. If I have trouble staying on task, a teacher may point to the "Stay on Task" card to remind me.

Isaak is doing so great in school. His teachers and family are so proud of him. Have a great year in school, Isaak!

Clothing Book

My name is Isaak. I have a body. I have a head and arms and legs and very nice eyes. All my body parts do different things. I wear different kinds of clothes for each part of my body.

Some clothes keep me warm. I can wear a hat and gloves and a scarf and a coat when it's real cold outside. I should always wear a coat when the weather is cooler. I can wear boots or take an umbrella when it rains. This keeps my body warm and protected.

I wear shoes and socks on my feet to protect them and keep them warm. Socks will keep my feet from STINKING! That's why I have to change my socks every day. I have to wear clean ones! Sometimes I can wear sandals when it's warm. Then, I don't need to wear socks.

I wear pants on my legs. I can wear sweats if I'm home or outside playing, but I should wear nicer pants like jeans or slacks to school. I wear suit pants to go to church. If it's warm, I can wear shorts. I always wear clean underwear. That's very important! No one likes a stinky bum!

I wear a shirt on my top. It covers my chest and my tummy, sometimes my arms. I wear long sleeves or a sweater if it's cold. I can wear short sleeves if it's warm outside. For church, I wear a nice shirt and a tie. That shows I'm respectful in the Lord's house. Some shirts have buttons. If I need help, I can ask, but first, I will try by myself.

Girls wear clothes, too. Their clothes can sometimes look the same like jeans or a t-shirt. But, most of the clothes they wear look a little different. That's because boys and girls are different, and they like different things, and their bodies are different. They might wear a dress or ballet shoes, and I don't wear those! They might have lace or ruffles. I don't wear those, either! But, girls look very nice, and I can tell them that. If a girl is wearing something pretty, I can say, "You look nice today!" She will like that.

I try to wear clothes that I feel comfortable in, but also make me look good. I wear clothes that are clean and clothes that look good together. I should try to match similar colors and patterns when I pick out my clothes.

Boys' and girls' bodies are different. Heavenly Father made us that way! It's wonderful! But, I must show respect and modesty. I need to dress in private. I need to remember to shut the door when I go to the bathroom or change clothes. If I get out of the shower and need to go to my room, I will wrap a towel around my body. If I have an accident, I will call out of the bathroom for help. I will not walk out of the bathroom naked. That is not being modest.

One reason for clothes is to cover our bodies. I shouldn't lift my shirt up in the air. I don't stick my hands down my pants. I also keep my hands out of other people's clothes, because they want to be modest, too.

These are all very important rules for clothing. Clothes keep me modest and private, but they can also be fun and express my personality. I will use good judgment to pick my clothes and will be modest each day. I feel good when I am well-dressed and clean!

Incentive Chart

The third book I created is not really a book at all but an incentive program. I include it here because it is a system that helps reinforce what the book is trying to teach. For Isaak, the Incentive Chart was sometimes an index card that reinforced what he was working on in a specific setting, usually taken from the Situation Book. Each expectation was listed, and he got a sticker or a checkmark if he followed it. There was always a reward at the end. Lavish praise and positive reinforcement helped him internalize and generalize these important social skills.

Good Behavior Card

A simple incentive program was sometimes all Isaak need to keep the rules fresh in his mind throughout the day.

Isaak's Good Behavior Card

Get a sticker at the end of the day for following all your Good Behavior Rules. We love you!

Get 10 stickers in a row and get a trip to your favorite burger bar!

School Day

Sometimes a more detailed reminder throughout the day was more helpful.

My Reward Checklist

☐ I listened in class.
☐ I played well with my friends.
☐ I went to my classes independently.
☐ I stayed on task.
☐ I completed my assignments.
☐ _____
☐ _____

If I get my checks, at the end of the day I get computer time!

Reward Chart

This program can be modified in any one of a number of ways. In this case, I created a large grid and every 10 to 15 squares wrote in a reward that Isaak enjoyed. The rewards included edibles like a bag of Goldfish, physical contact like rough-housing with Dad, mone-

Bag of Goldfish				
			$5	
	Game Boy game			

tary rewards, and an occasional big reward like a new Game Boy game. Throughout the day, I would acknowledge good behaviors and social skills that Isaak was demonstrating, and for each he would get to put a sticker on a square. Many stickers were given each day, and generous praise was included.

Rewards Jar

I printed a list of activities and rewards that Isaak enjoyed and cut them out separately. The list of rewards included rent a game, baseball cards, McDonald's trip, play game with Mom or Dad, trip to a book store, Xbox time, and so forth. These were given when Isaak had done something extraordinarily well. For example, if he

offered to help his sister with something without being asked or if he came home with a glowing report from school, I would say, "Wow! You did such-and-such so nicely. You earned a reward!" and he would jump up and down and get to pick one out of the jar.

Behavior Ladder

This was a system we used at school when Isaak's behavior had become a problem and we needed to get him back on track. I had him sit down with me and list all his favorite things to have and do. I then had him prioritize them in order of importance to him. I created the ladder and put the least favorite at the bottom and the most favorite at the top. He took it to school with him each day. At the end of each school day, his teacher would

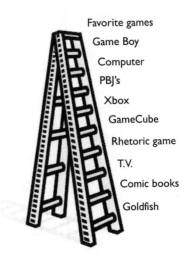

Favorite games
Game Boy
Computer
PBJ's
Xbox
GameCube
Rhetoric game
T.V.
Comic books
Goldfish

evaluate his day with him and inform him if he moved up or down on the ladder. When we first started this program, we had him start at the bottom and work his way up. In other words, for the first few days, he had little to do at home. He had to be creative. It was great! And he was highly motivated to move up so his behavior made a big turnaround very quickly.

Portable Goal Sheet

This was also something his teachers were able to use. I found mini-clipboards at a store, small enough for the teacher to put around her neck and keep discreetly. I reviewed the selected goals with Isaak before using the system. He knew that making a goal got him a check in the box, and for every eight checks, he earned a reward. He had a separate piece of paper with all his goals written on it that he kept with him, taped on his notebook.

Flexible					**Goal!**
Listen					**Goal!**
Find out					**Goal!**
Compromise					**Goal!**
Control self					**Goal!**

My Goals:

1. I will be flexible in my school activities and in my play with my friends.

2. I will listen and respond to my friends' conversation and interests.

3. I will find out more about my friends by asking them questions.

4. I will find things to do with my friends that they want to do and make compromises if I need to.

5. I will appropriately handle difficult situations.

I'm finding as Isaak gets older and continues to improve that I use these books less frequently. I can now talk to him about situations and have him understand without much written support. His language and development is also now such that he can understand more of the *whys* behind what is asked of him. We are able to discuss situations that come up in the same manner that I have been able to do with my typical daughter all these years. His understanding of the *reasons* has finally caught up with his ability to *comply* with the expectations, but in the early years, he just needed to know the expectations, and once he knew them, he made great progress.

These techniques will not work for every child. Some children may not need such concrete examples and expectations laid out for them. If they don't, that's great! There are other techniques out there that can help promote better social understanding than these may. The purpose of these books is merely to tap into the strength and interest of the child with hyperlexia. Children with hyperlexia may be too young to comprehend the larger social reasons when these techniques are most useful which is in the very early years. With that said, these individualized books could possibly make a huge difference and are certainly worth a try. You will know by the fruits of your labors if your child begins changing his behavior for the better after introducing them.

Chapter 7

Navigating the School System

Before I had children, I had this image of what the first day of school would be like. I'd dress up my child in a cute outfit, put his backpack on him, take some pictures, shed a few tears, and send him on his way. If only it was that simple! Sending your child to school each day is truly taken for granted until you have a child with special needs. In that case, it becomes a constant struggle, invariable heart-ache, and even when you think things are going well, a new problem occurs. I had no idea how much there was to know when we started this journey. Know your child, know your options, and know your rights. Each country and each local government and even each community's resources will be different. My knowledge of special education law is limited to the situation in the US—if you live in a different country, I'd suggest contacting your government's education department. This chapter is based on my experiences in the US, so bear in mind that your school system may differ. I've included legal information about special education law in the US in Appendix A, as well as some useful contacts for readers in the UK in Appendix B. Knowing what the law entails is certainly the first step, but actually *using* that information to benefit your child is the key.

Placement

Finding an appropriate educational placement for your child may be one of your biggest challenges. You will have several options to choose from, depending on your child's age and the school's available classes.

Birth to three years old

Before age three, there is generally less regulation on what your school district must provide. Services to address your child's needs may differ from district to district. Some districts offer a fully functioning preschool class where your child will not only get services (such as speech and OT), but will also have opportunities for good social interaction and learning to handle a classroom setting. Other districts offer their services at a center, but no organized preschool is provided. Still others have therapists come to the child's home to work with him there. When Isaak was that age, the local birth-to-three center offered a program which included two days a week small group preschool (four to five boys, all challenged in some way). It was great, but I felt Isaak needed more group learning and social interaction, so I called the next nearest birth-to-three center and found out they also had a two-day-a-week class. I asked if I could sign Isaak up for both, and they agreed. Between the two centers, Isaak had four mornings a week, two hours a day, in a social group setting, targeting those goals. I had him in private and home therapy the rest of the day.

Three to five years old

When your child turns three, school districts may be required to provide services in a preschool setting free of charge. Although each district is required to provide preschool, the classes offered vary widely from school to school. You will need to observe what classes are available to him. Some of the options include the following.

Highly structured program

There may be an autism spectrum disorder or similar classroom. These classrooms will be highly structured. They run on a regular schedule. They may use picture or text schedules with the children so they know what is coming next to lessen transition difficulties. There is usually a higher teacher-to-child ratio. Besides the special education teacher, there may be more aides in this class than in the other preschool classrooms. In some cases, there will be a one-on-one ratio of a more rigorous form, working on individual goals each day. If your child is more impaired or needs lots of structure to learn, then this classroom may be appropriate. This usually is the case in the early years when less language has been acquired and behavior is still a challenge. Once your child becomes more attuned to his environment, putting him into a less restrictive environment may be more appropriate.

Early childhood class

There may be a special education classroom that serves children with all disabilities. This program may be broken down into smaller groups depending upon the degree of behavioral challenge or medical fragility, but often all children will be educated together. Many school districts will include typical children in this program to give the children with disabilities good peer models. Many children qualify for this program with speech delays or physical challenges. They may be typical children that need some assistance to catch up with their peers. Some children come with more severe physical or mental disabilities. There is often a mix of disabilities. The quality and level of this program varies with each school district and each classroom. If your child only needs minor assistance to function in a classroom setting and is able to respond to peers and learn in a less restrictive environment, this may be a good place to enroll. You should visit the available options before committing to the program.

Private social preschool

You may choose to send your child to a private preschool. If you find a class with an understanding and loving teacher and a classroom that seems to fit your child's unique style, then this may be a good choice. Perhaps a regular preschool setting that focuses on free play and social engagement would be your choice. Many preschools have social and behavior skills as their main goal. If you have a child that is more impaired, but you feel a typical preschool would benefit him, you may need to send your own trained aide to attend with him. The aide can be there to help him engage, learn how to play with the kids, follow instructions, pinpoint problem areas, and can probably do this much better than the teacher alone can. Having an extra pair of hands in the classroom might be appreciated.

Private academic preschool

Perhaps you think a more academic program may be beneficial. After all, your child thrives on academics. In this environment, your child may feel confident and safe. He may be more inclined to be socially engaging and behaviorally in-tune because he's in a setting in which he's comfortable. Especially if he is allowed and even encouraged to move at his own pace and learn new things, he may be more responsive. However, beware that he is not allowed to disappear into his own world. That is certainly a risk. If you have a teacher aware of the situation and taught how to help him engage, it might be just the place for him.

Elementary school age

From the time your child is elementary age (five or six), your child will most likely be educated at your home school. At this point, a regular education teacher needs to be involved in your child's education if he is to participate in the general education program. Most children with hyperlexia do. Taking into consideration your child's age, his level of functioning, and your school's options, you can make an educated choice.

Classroom choice

Once your child is ready for kindergarten your classroom choices change slightly. There may be a self-contained special education classroom where the children all have some level of a disability. Usually the class will be very small with a high teacher–student ratio. The children in this class most likely will be affected by their disability in such a way that they cannot participate in the regular education classroom. Some districts offer an integrated classroom where the number of special education students and typical students are fairly balanced. There is usually a special education teacher and a general education teacher with additional aides in the classroom as needed. There will also be the general education classroom. This will be a typical classroom where your child could be anywhere from the only one on an IEP to one of many. It depends on the number of students with special needs that year.

Teacher choice

Often the best choice comes down to picking the teacher. A good teacher can make almost any situation successful, and a bad teacher can ruin even the best classroom situation. Before you make a final decision on the placement for your child, get to know the teachers that are available. You can get a good feel for teachers' strengths and weaknesses by doing a few things. You can go and observe the teachers during teaching time. See how they run their classrooms. See if they are organized and have good instructional control. See if the kids like them and respond to them. If you can, spend some time after school hours or during recess talking with them. Find out what their philosophies are, how they run their classrooms, how they deal with behavior challenges, and how successful they are at integrating children with special needs. Find out if they are willing to make accommodations such as writing out instructions and giving other written prompts. Find out if they are prepared to accommodate a child with unusually high abilities as well as special needs. A teacher of a child with hyperlexia should abandon any preconceived notions and will need to be prepared to do things they'd never considered before.

Pull-out services

Your child may need some special assistance, whether it is speech or occupational therapy or academic support. These services will be provided during school hours. Your child will be pulled out of his regular class to receive these services. If you are concerned that your child should appear as typical as possible, you may ask that these services be provided at a time when it's not so obvious to the rest of the class that he is being pulled out. It might be the second half of the long lunch recess or the first 30 minutes of the day or some other time that can be discreet. If he's working on social goals, perhaps they could pull out another typical child or two with whom to work.

Aide support

Many children with hyperlexia have sufficient challenges, especially in the early years, to warrant extra support in the classroom. They are not impaired enough to need a self-contained classroom, but in order to be successful in the general education classroom, they need more support.

This can be achieved in a variety of ways. This could be anything from a full-time dedicated aide to a part-time shared aide. The goal is to, first, help your child be successful in the classroom and, second, appear as typical as possible. Make sure the aide is well-trained. When in doubt, feel free to bring in your own training staff to achieve this. A poorly trained aide can be worse than no aide at all. If you are working towards your child's full independence in the classroom, everyone on the team should be aware that the teacher is the primary line of defense, and the aide is the secondary. The teacher should know all the strategies to use and should step in to assist the child as much as possible, and the aide can either step in to help other students as needed or step in to help your child when the teacher is unable. Tell them that the aide's job is to work herself or himself out of a job.

Modifications and accommodations

Even when you have a good classroom and teacher situation, you may be required to ask for special modifications for your child to be successful. These modifications vary greatly depending on the child's needs and each unique situation. As time goes on, you will need to modify the modifications, as your child's needs will be changing constantly. Keep on top of his progress and be prepared to make regular changes.

Visual accommodations

Because your child responds so well to visual cues, you will need to help your school staff use this skill. It is not uncommon to find that in the early school years, most of the instruction given to students is given orally. Most kids do not read early, and even if they do, they can still learn aurally (by hearing), so most teachers teach by talking. Your child's ability to absorb information may be primarily visual. Ask teachers to write out instructions for your child if he is struggling to follow. He could have a small notebook or sticky-notes on his desk just for this purpose. When the teacher has finished giving instructions to the entire class, he or she can quickly write the same directions down at your child's desk. This will not only give him a chance to understand and follow the instruction, but he can do so independently with the note to refer to. Checklists are also useful. These can be used before or after a task. Your child can have a checklist with instructions to do this, this, and this, or for him to check that he did do this, this, and this. You can also send notes to your child from home in his backpack or lunchbox. This can be just a love-note from mom or an encouraging note or even a reminder to do something or work on a certain goal. It may be just the thing he needs in the middle of the day. Written prompts also work on the playground to encourage social interaction or to work on specific goals. If your child responds to such visual accommodations, use them!

Gifted accommodations

You will probably find that encouraging your child in areas in which he excels will yield good results behaviorally and socially. When he is confident and comfortable (as he may be when he is working on something stimulating) he may be more responsive and adjusted to his environment. For example, math is where Isaak shines. He loves it and is extremely talented. Instead of keeping him in his grade for math class, he has been sent to upper grades for that class. As a result, he has rarely had any behavior problems in math class. He is attentive and responsive to instruction. He looks the most "typical" in math than at any other time at school, even though he is in class with kids four years older than he is. Children with hyperlexia generally have high intellectual abilities. Just because your child may struggle with language or social or behavioral expectations does not mean his intellectual potential is compromised. You want to stimulate and teach him in areas in which he struggles, but don't neglect his gifts.

Verbal accommodations

Your child may have language processing difficulties. He may have a hard time understanding verbal language or deciphering underlying meanings. He may misunderstand non-verbal cues or not be able to express himself well. Ask his teachers to learn to model language for him. Show his teachers how to talk to him. Teach them to ask your child to repeat back instructions. It is not uncommon for a child with hyperlexia to say he understands an instruction when he doesn't, either to get out of the task at hand or because he doesn't understand what the response to the instruction should be. When an instruction is given, have the teacher ask him to repeat it back. Your child may be receiving private speech and language therapy, but he may also qualify for therapy at school. If you haven't done so already, check into it. The therapist at school can work with your child one-on-one, but there is a lot of opportunity for peer-learning at school. The therapist can choose peers to join the therapy session and, as such, your child will have good verbal models to learn from.

Social accommodations

Becoming socially adept may be one of your child's biggest challenges. There are so many social intricacies to learn that may not come naturally. School is an excellent place to work on these skills. Your child will be inundated with social opportunities in the classroom as well as on the playground. If done appropriately, a buddy program can be successful. It is often a task that other kids in the classroom seek after—to be the "buddy" at recess time. As your child gets older and more socially advanced, have his teachers encourage friendships as they begin to emerge. Your child may be able to function well in a casual setting such as on the playground, but he may struggle with forming deeper friendships. If teachers can identify someone with whom your child may be able to connect or identify someone with whom he is spending regular time, they may be able to encourage that and help your child gain those important social reciprocity skills. Do not neglect social goals when constructing your child's IEP.

Looking "typical"

If your child functions well in a typical setting, it may be important to foster that "normalcy." If he is capable, you may want your child to act and be treated like everyone else. He deserves that! In the early years, most typical kids do not consider differences as undesirable. Sadly, that mentality changes as they get older, and the fact that your child struggles with language or social expectations or that he is receiving special help may be to his detriment. There are things your child's teachers can do to minimize that dilemma. If your child has a certain goal, the teachers can find other students in the class to also work on that goal. If the teachers need to correct your child regularly on a behavior, they may be able to find other students who also need the same guidance. The speech therapist can ask to work with your child only in a group setting so the other students do not know who is targeted. This effort will help your child blend in as much as possible and be treated like all the other students in his class.

A word about labels and integration

I have never been a fan of the term "a child with a disability," and yet that is the term used in school and in our society to refer to children with unique needs. I much prefer a child with a challenge or a difference. Although I do not choose this hill to die on, I have tried to the best of my ability and opportunities to educate people around me that these children are just that—children. Every child is different and every child has varying needs. Some children require more assistance to learn than others, but some require less. I am not afraid of the word "autism" or "hyperlexia" any more than I am of "red hair" or "short." All children, if they are able, have the right to be educated with, to play with, and to grow up with other children of all diversity. Try not to be in denial about your child's special needs, but also make sure he is treated with the utmost respect and educated with other typical children to the fullest extent possible.

When you have to fight

It is to be hoped you will be able to find a good placement for your child, have teachers who educate in your child's best interest, and have a smooth transition from year to year. That will not always be the case. When it isn't, do your best to maintain a good relationship with your school personnel. It is easier to catch flies with honey! I have found that something as simple as bringing treats to meetings, sending thank-you notes, or having a non-school, personal relationship with a key member on the IEP team has gone a long way when a conflict arises. Even so, there may be a time when an agreement cannot be obtained. When an issue arises, you need to be educated. If you know your rights, know what is worth fighting for and what is not, and do so in a pleasant but steadfast manner, you will be a step ahead.

Process guidelines

Having gone through the process myself, I know that getting information from others who have gone through it is important. The following is some advice from other parents who have hoed the row before you.

Read the literature

The school may give you legal information at your meetings. In the United States, they are required to give Procedural Safeguards at every meeting. These explain all of your rights under the law including independent educational evaluations, access to school records, confidentiality of records, and complaints against the educational agency. Know your rights and what recourse you have if a problem arises.

Know the law

Educate yourself on all parts of the law in your area, pertinent to your situation. I've found that learning about the law has not only helped me with the education of my own child, but has made it possible for me to help other parents who may not have learned that information yet. You can be a great force of good for more than your own child by being educated on the law and regulations in your area.

Bring your own professionals to the meetings

The school has to balance the needs of your child with the needs of all the other children in the class and at school. Your only concern is your own child and that his needs are being met. Bringing private professionals who have evaluated or worked your child and have an objective opinion can help you further his cause. You can also bring someone as a support to your meetings. Someone else might be more objective or think of other questions to ask that may elude you. It is nice to have someone with whom you can discuss the meeting afterwards.

Have thorough evaluations done

Allow the school to do whatever evaluations they see fit, but if possible get private evaluations done as well. If both sets of evaluations are in line with each other, then you have that second opinion and you can move forward. If they are not, you can try to figure out why there is a discrepancy and where to go from there. Do not make the mistake of accepting a placement or a service without the assessments to back it up. If you do not agree with the results of the school's assessments, you can ask for further evaluations. You have the right to obtain an independent evaluation at public expense if you disagree with the results of the school's assessment. This evaluation cannot be done by someone employed by the school district. It must be objective.

Keep a paper trail

Keep a file of all the paperwork that goes back and forth from your school district. Keep a copy of any letter you send to them. Make any important requests to your school district in writing, and ask that they respond in writing. Keeping a phone log of dates and conversation topics can also be useful if a conflict arises. It's better to have more information than you will ever need to use than to not have the information you do need if a problem arises.

Request the results

Request the school's evaluation and assessment results prior to any meeting. This will give you a chance to read over them and compare them with your own private results. It is also considerate to provide your evaluation and assessment results to the school before the meeting.

Create high-quality goals

In creating goals for your child, make sure the goals are measurable and reachable. Do not agree to goals that you know will be achieved in the next month nor to goals that you can't imagine your child ever making. Each goal needs to have a way of measuring your child's progress that could, if necessary, be transferred to a new school district who would then be able to pick up where the old district left off.

Work as a team

See your school as an essential partner. Even if a conflict arises, be assertive but respectful. Your school undoubtedly has experience to back up their suggestions. You do know your child best, but realize that they have good information. Be open with your school personnel. Don't hide information from them. Having open lines of communication will foster a good relationship.

Educate

Don't shy away from educating your school district if you have information they do not. No one, not even a school district, knows everything. If you know more about your child's disorder or have more information about the law of which they are not aware, feel free to share that. I've found that even people who are supposed to be in-the-know like to have more information if given to them in a respectful, working-together manner.

Be persistent

Keep the meeting going until your child gets what he needs. A meeting does not have to be done in the time allotted if there is more to be discussed. Even if you do have to close a meeting, you can call for another one to be arranged before you end. The process may take work. Do not expect everything to be resolved in one fell swoop and fall into place perfectly. Just like parenting, educating can be hard work!

Keep the end goal in mind

Where do you want to see your child in three months? In a year? In five years? Do you have a good idea of where you want him to go? What he is capable of? Thinking about long-term outcomes will help you create good short-term objectives.

Stay calm and professional

This is so important. Keeping yourself calm and clear and stating your ideas or requests in a matter-of-fact manner is helpful. Nothing can be gained by losing your cool or ranting and raving. It will only make the school district defensive and create an atmosphere of conflict.

Chapter 8

Customizing Behavior Therapy

Applied Behavior Analysis, or ABA, has come to be one of the most popular and research-based therapies for children with autism. ABA is a system of breaking down skills into small, manageable pieces, teaching each minute skill with positive reinforcement, building upon already learned skills, and teaching the child to then use those skills as a typical child would—in the real world.

B.F. Skinner (1998) is perhaps the grandfather of today's behavior therapy. His work studied operant conditioning in which the consequence of behavior controls the future occurrence of the behavior. In simple terms, a behavior occurs and a reinforcer is given that will increase the likelihood of that behavior occurring again. It comes down to shaping behavior and rewiring the brain.

If Skinner is the grandfather, then Ivar Lovaas is the father of today's ABA (Lovaas 1987; Lovaas and Smith 2003). In the 1960s and 1970s, Lovaas began working on a curriculum of behavioral programs to help children with autism improve their language, behavior, and social skills. His program was intense, but nearly 50 percent of the children involved showed remarkable progress. This was the first application of the science of behavior analysis used to teach individuals with autism.

An ABA program can have a variety of components such as social skills training, self-help skills training, language therapy, and so forth. An ABA program should be overseen by a professional consultant who can help train you or anyone you have tutoring your child.

The purpose of this chapter is not to detail ABA nor how to get a program running. There is plenty of literature available to fulfill that need. Instead, this chapter might give you ideas about how to modify some common ABA programs in working with a child with hyperlexia. This is not a full curriculum, but it will, it is hoped, get you going on a path towards better customizing your child's current therapies to make full benefit of his particular abilities.

Pro-active responses

It is important to remember that positive reinforcement and pro-active responses will help your child progress.

Behavior specific praise

Your child should frequently receive behavior specific praise for appropriate behavior. *Behavior specific* means instead of saying, "Good job" you say, "Good sitting in your seat" or "Thank you for standing in line patiently." This should be delivered as soon as possible after the correct behavior occurs. There can never be too much positive praise! A good rule of thumb is to praise your child three times for every correction. As he gets older and in a natural setting, try not to "hover" over him. If you are unable to deliver praise immediately, remember to address it at a later time when it's more appropriate.

Reinforcement system

Use whatever is most motivating for your child. ABA managers and tutors often use edible treats in the early stages as rewards. That may not be motivating to your child. Letters might! Instead of using treats, you can give letter stickers or write the numbers for him. As he gets older, you'll find other things that motivate him. Make him work for what he wants most. He will be motivated to learn valuable skills this way. We have gone through a variety of reinforcement systems including token economies (working for a predetermined number of tokens in order to gain desired object or activity), charts (letter sticker for every correct targeted behavior), coupons (earning minutes on the computer for each correct targeted behavior), and a variety of other systems. Find what your child responds to and use it in a reinforcement system for him.

General prompting

Use written or verbal prompts to help your child learn appropriate behavior. Prompts should be direct or indirect. Once he responds appropriately to a direct prompt, an indirect prompt can be used. An example of a direct prompt is: "Remember to look at your friend when you are talking to him;" and of an indirect prompt is: "Don't forget what to do when you talk to your friends."

Verbal "prep"

If you know your child will be entering a situation that could cause inflexibility, provide a clear written or verbal warning or rule indicating what might happen and how he should behave. If he is about to enter a situation requiring complex or multiple step task completion, provide a simple explanation indicating the steps that he will be required to take. If possible, have him repeat the steps back to you before he begins the task.

Rule cards

If necessary, create rule cards (simple rules) listed on index cards that can be used as visuals to remind your child of what is expected during specific situations. These should be shown to him just prior to entering the situation.

Prompt fading

It's important to fade any prompts that you use as soon as possible. This will help avoid prompt-dependence (not doing a task that he can do without your prompt). Go from direct to indirect prompting, and then fade your proximity to him. Be creative in coming up with ways to fade out prompts completely. For example, "You need to ask your friends three questions while you are in the cafeteria today. Then, I'll give you a point;" to "Remember, three for a point;" to holding up three fingers for him to see before going in; to no reminders.

Redirect

If your child is showing signs of frustration, attempt to redirect him as soon as possible by making a short comment and drawing his attention away from the trigger. Many problems can be avoided by this method.

Use obsessions

Know what your child responds to most and use that in your teaching. We have made Isaak work for letter stickers, Pokemon cards, and a chance to do math. We have been known to make Who Wants To Be a Millionaire and Jeopardy! games for targeted skills. Some people have children who love to chew on straws or twirl their hair or jump on the trampoline obsessively. Research has shown that working for such obsessions should not increase the obsession, and it should allow for better results during the task (Charlop-Christy and Haymes 1998).

Foundation skills

It might seem obvious, but in order for your child to learn, he has to be "prepared to learn." A child jumping out of his chair, yelling, and looking out the window is probably not a child that is going to respond well to direct teaching. A child sitting in his chair, looking at you, and anticipating learning because he knows it will be fun and motivating is going to go far! This is instructional control, and with it, your child will make progress. In the beginning, his obsession with letters and the written word may be what most helps him learn to attend to instruction and respond. Once he can do that, you can then use those visual abilities to actually teach him important skills.

Attending skills

Sitting

Purpose: To come to the table when called and sit in preparation for instruction.

Prepare some of your child's favorite interests and have them at the table. We used letter stickers, letter stamps, foam letters, and letter cookies in those early months. The letters were most effective at the time because Isaak was interested in them and wanted them to be produced one after the other, so he was able to work for longer periods of time with letters than with any other reinforcer. Once you have something that will motivate your child, call his name and say, "Come sit." Wait five seconds. If he does not begin to respond, walk over to him and say again, "Come sit" and help him stand up and walk over to his chair and sit down. Ignore any protestations. Once he is sitting, say, "Good sitting!" and give him the reinforcement. Continue this program until he independently comes when called.

Hands down

Purpose: To put hands in lap when requested.

When your child is sitting in the chair but his hands are not in his lap, say, "Hands down." If he does not respond within five seconds, say it again, and then hand-over-hand put his hands in his lap. Say, "Good putting hands down" and give the reinforcement. This should first be done at a time when he's not in trouble for having his hands all over the place so as to teach him the expectation with a good feeling. Once he knows what's expected, you can use this instruction any time you need him to be still and attending to you. This can be modified for any other distracting mannerism.

Pointing

Purpose: To point to something when requested.

Use something motivating like a sheet with randomized alphabet letters or numbers or a favorite book with a variety of pictures on a page. Tell your child to "Point to 'L,'" for example. If he does not respond within five seconds, say it again, and hand-over-hand help him point to the correct response and give the reinforcement saying, "Good pointing!" Continue until he will point independently when asked. Once he can point to a book or something on paper, teach him to point to things in space. You can place his favorite letters on a shelf and have him "Point to 'L'" there.

Imitation

Purpose: To imitate upon command.

You can modify any standard imitation program (with objects, gross motor, fine motor, oral motor) to be more adaptable to your child's interests. Choosing objects of interest, such as letters, to work with can be more effective. Make sure he is attending to you, then say, "Do this," and then put the letter in the box or clap your hands or open your mouth wide. If he doesn't respond within five seconds, say it again, and hand-over-hand prompt him to do it, then give the reinforcement. If he is able to read at this point, it may help to give him the written cue along with the verbal request.

Making a choice

Purpose: To learn to make a choice between at least two options.

Once your child can make a choice, he will be more able to handle transitions and changes and will be more compliant. You can turn almost anything into a choice so that he has some control in his life. Prepare index cards with pictures and/or words with your child's favorite things. Have a few cards for food items, a few for toys, a few for videos, etc. Before you give him one of the items, present him with the appropriate card and have him read it. Say, "Good choosing *apple*," for example, and give him the chosen item. Once he regularly reads the card, present him with a choice between the preferred item and a non-preferred item—an apple card and a spoon card. Once he can choose between those consistently, present him with a choice between two preferred items. Continue making it more complex, and use fewer and fewer written cues and more verbal requests for making a choice.

Social skills
Social eye contact—learning when to "check in"

Purpose: To learn when to look at another person when engaged in a shared activity.

Prior to engaging in the activity, your child's eye contact should be primed. Create social scripts or rule sheets so that specific joint attention statements are paired with looking at your communicative partner. The script could say, "When you say, 'What do you think?' or 'I see _____ too,' or 'Look at _____,' you need to look at me." Read over this story before you begin the activity.

You should engage in a shared activity such as looking at a book, playing a game, or completing an art project. During the activity, be sure to make the same target statements presented to your child as you wrote in the story, and also be sure that you make eye contact with your child when you make those statements. When your child makes the target statements paired with eye contact, use behavior-specific praise to reinforce his eye contact. "Wow! You looked at me when you said, 'I've drawn a truck.'" If he does not pair eye contact with a target phrase, you should draw his attention to the rules sheet and ask him to practice. Be sure to change the target phrases to match the joint activity at hand.

Emotions

Purpose: To increase ability to understand and show appropriate emotions.

Create a worksheet with two columns. Title one column "Situation/Cause" and the other, "Emotion." Think of some simple situations such as "I lost my doll" and "I got a new bike." Write those down on the left-hand side. On the right-hand side, randomly draw a face with an emotion (happy, sad, angry). Present the worksheet to your child. Read over the situations and prompt him to draw a line to the appropriate emotion face. Create new situations each time. This program can be made as simple (happy, sad, angry) or as complex (confused, embarrassed) as your child needs to learn.

Interactive games

Purpose: To learn to play a variety of interactive games.

Provide your child with a list of basic rules for an interactive game such as soccer or tag. Once he can independently state the rules, set up a game in which the rules will need to be applied, and begin playing. If at any time your child does not follow the rules, review the rules with him. Give him an opportunity to follow the rule independently. If he needs it, provide him with a small "cheat sheet" of the rules of the game to keep in his pocket. He may not need to refer to it during the game, but just knowing it is there may help him remember to follow the rules.

Pretend play

Purpose: To engage in multiple imaginative play activities and pretend to be a variety of characters.

Introduce an imaginative play activity such as cowboys, pirates, or firefighters. Say, "It's time to play _____. Pretend you're a _____." If he does not begin to respond, model appropriate play, and he should imitate your actions. Books or videos can be used as models to illustrate how particular characters behave, materials they use or wear, and places where they live or visit. Give him written cues if necessary.

Observational learning

Purpose: To engage in activities by observing peers in the environment.

Set up a situation where two peers are engaged in a play activity. Your child should be told to watch his friends play. After a specific amount of time elapses, approach him and ask him how to play the observed game. If he does not know, instruct him to observe his peers again. Provide verbal prompts, walking him through the rules of the game as he observes. When he can tell you how to play the game, he should be told to join. If at any time he does not follow the rules of the game, he should be taken aside and asked to state the rules again. This program can be made as simple (pushing a car back and forth, throwing a ball in a basket) or as complex (freeze tag, kickball) as your child needs to learn.

Phone conversation

Purpose: To learn appropriate phone conversation behavior.

Set up a role playing game where you and your child engage in a conversation over the phone. He should be learning that the voice on the other end of the phone is coming from an actual person, so begin by having both of you in the same room. Next, you step out of the room but continue talking on the phone. The distance between you and your child should gradually increase. If at any time he does not engage in a conversation appropriately, provide verbal or textual prompting. Some target phone behaviors should be answering questions, waiting for the other person to finish speaking before he begins talking, and responding to comments.

Asking others about their activity or product

Purpose: During a structured activity, to request information about what peers are doing while engaged with them.

This program should be done after your child can already share what he has made or what he is doing with adults and peers in his environment. The purpose of this program is to help him request information about what his peers are doing. When you see your child making eye contact with another person during play, model for him an appropriate query such as, "What are you drawing?" Use textual prompts as needed, but be discreet so as not to interrupt social interaction. Be sure to reinforce his commenting in these situations so that he will continue to make comments and seek attention for his own actions and objects.

Social interaction

Purpose: To improve social interaction skills.

Present your child with rules for one of the targeted social behaviors. For example, state, "When you want to talk to someone, you must first get that person's attention. What do you do first?" Once he can independently state these rules, set up role playing activities in which the rules will need to be applied. Role playing activities can be set up using puppets, figures, or actual people. Multiple scenarios should be provided so that your child is able to practice behaving appropriately in a variety of situations. If at any time he does not use appropriate social behaviors, stop the activity and have him review the rules. After the rule has been reviewed, give your child the opportunity to apply the rules to the scenario again.

Problem solving

Role-playing appropriate behavior

Purpose: To improve social situational behavior through role playing and practice.

Present your child with a written set of rules for a targeted social behavior. He should then be asked questions pertaining to the rules such as, "What should you do if someone calls you a name?" Once he can correctly answer the questions, present role playing activities with puppets or figures in which the rules will need to be applied. Provide opportunity to practice using the targeted behavior in a variety of novel situations. Some examples: What would you do if someone cut in line? What would you do if someone pushed you out on the playground? What would you do if you wanted to play with something someone else had? What would you do if you wanted to join in someone's game?

Real life situations

Purpose: To identify a real life problem and state what is needed to resolve the problem.

Create obvious problem situations for your child to identify, e.g., state that it is time to go for a bike ride and, when your child gets to the bike, the tires will be flat. When presented with the problem situation, your child should identify what is wrong with the item/situation and state why it is a problem and what could be done to fix the problem.

If your child makes a mistake or fails to respond, provide him with visual cues such as photographs or symbols from which he could choose. In the above example, if he does not tell you that the tires need air or that they need a pump, you could provide him with several visual options from which to choose, such as a picture of full tires with the textual cue "tires need air" and several other distractors.

Academic skills

Although your child may not need academic help in the beginning, you can use his academic prowess to teach him other skills. As already introduced, he may be more motivated to learn to point by pointing to letters, he may be better equipped to handle transitions if he can tell the time, and he may be more inclined to do artwork if you have letter stamps. Be creative and use his skills to your advantage.

Because your child is talented in academic ways, it may be that he will deal with boredom at school. Prevent this occurrence as much as possible by finding a good school placement for him. However, there will be times, for whatever reason, when he will need to sit and attend to instruction that is well below his ability level. We all have to sit through that boring meeting from time to time. Teaching him appropriate behavior in such a situation can be important as he gets older.

As your child gets older, it's possible that he may struggle with handwriting, story writing, or reading comprehension. Many children with hyperlexia do. Here are some ideas.

Maintaining attention

Purpose: To attend to a peer or an adult for a non-preferred activity while in the presence of distracting items or activities.

Your child should be placed in a situation where he is required to attend to an adult or a peer (e.g., begin a conversation with him, listening to instructions or a story). A distracting item or activity should be placed in close proximity to where he is sitting (such as a calendar, a calculator, a computerized device). Before the adult or peer begins to speak, tell your child that he will earn points for keeping his attention on the speaker. These points should be given for keeping his hands off of the item, keeping his eyes on the person talking, asking questions about the person's topic, and making contingent statements about the person's topic. If he attends to the speaker for the duration of time determined, he should receive a point. If at any time he becomes distracted, he should be redirected and told that he will not receive a point at that time. Once the time has elapsed, the distracting item or activity should be removed from the situation. If he maintains attention for the entire trial, he should receive access to an additional reinforcer.

Handwriting

Purpose: To improve handwriting skills.

Prepare a list of written rules for good handwriting skills and have the rules posted somewhere obvious.

This program should be taught in a highly motivating manner. For example, have him choose an activity in which he would like to participate. Have him pick a simple sentence to write pertaining to the activity such as "I like to play video games." A timer should then be set for a specific amount of time. He should spend the entire duration of time writing the specific sentence. The letters should be written on the provided line slowly and neatly. After the timer sounds, he should receive a point for each letter written appropriately. Points can then be traded in for a certain amount of time with the desired activity (i.e., one point = one minute). This program can be made as simple (short sentence provided) or as complex (full paragraph) as your child needs to learn.

Handwriting Rules

1. Keep my letters on the line.
2. Write small so I can fit all my words on my paper.
3. Remember a space between each word.
4. Write slowly and neatly.

Academic writing

Purpose: To improve academic writing skills.

A variety of writing activities should be printed up and cut apart. Introduce each activity before your child is asked to write about it independently. Put the activities in a bag from which your child can pick. Use a timer, and have him write for that time. A reward should be given for good writing. Remember, this is a writing assignment, not a handwriting assignment. Although neat handwriting is important, teaching him good writing skills is the primary focus of his program. Some examples of writing activities are:

- writing a personal page
- writing a poem
- writing a short story
- drawing a story
- writing an essay
- doing a vocabulary page
- writing a letter
- writing a report
- copying dictation
- writing a dialogue
- making a sentence diagram
- typing.

Story writing

Purpose: To improve creative writing abilities.

Help your child write imaginative stories. The curriculum in *Teach Me Language* (Freeman, Dake, and Tamir 1997) is good for this purpose. If your child struggles to generate ideas, help him by providing him with a word bank or scripted choices. This should not be about a past experience or previously read book, but it should be an imaginative and logically sequenced original story.

Summarizing

Purpose: To summarize a story in the effort to improve reading comprehension.

You or your child should read a short story. After the story is completed, your child should be instructed to summarize the story using a specific number of sentences. For example, state, "What was the story about? Use two sentences to tell me." If he does not respond correctly, provide him with choices of appropriate ways to summarize. Begin with one sentence, and then increase the length and number and complexity as he improves. Teach him to summarize content in his own words. Start by teaching him to note the important words in the passage. He should be able to do this when someone reads to him and when he reads to himself.

Chapter 9

Customizing Language Therapy

A large percentage of all our programs over the years have been dedicated to improving Isaak's language skills. Language involves the ability to understand language, to use language, and to make understandable sounds, and there are lots of complex, higher-level skills to gain. At first, language is concrete—nouns and simple sentences—which can be fairly simple to teach. As your child's language skills increase, the teaching of higher-level skills will become more challenging.

Receptive language
Read and point

Purpose: To increase receptive vocabulary.

Prepare cards with pictures of common people, body parts, food, animals, etc. At first, write the words on the cards together with the pictures. Start with one card on the table at a time. "Point to *ball*." If he does not respond, say it again, and then hand-over-hand help him point to the picture of the ball, and offer reinforcement. When he can do that, add another card to the table. When he understands the concept and is complying, and once he is consistently pointing to several pictures, take the words off the pictures, and continue the program.

Following instructions

Purpose: To follow simple instructions upon command.

From the most elementary one-step directions to complex, multi-task steps, instructions to your child can be modified to utilize his reading skills. Following the same ABA procedure (give command, wait, prompt if needed, reinforce), couple the request with a written prompt. Start with simple instructions such as "Give ball" or "Read book." Gradually add more words to your instructions and then add additional steps such as "Give me the book and then sit down." Fade the written prompts as soon as you can.

Differentiating verbal sounds

Purpose: To be able to differentiate different sounds in speech.

Present your child with two index cards with words that have similar sounds (e.g., bat and brat; thirteen and thirty). Pick words whose sounds your child struggles to hear the difference. Having him "see" the sounds should help him to learn to differentiate between them. Prompt him to point to the words on command.

Expressive language
Yes and no

Purpose: To use Yes and No appropriately.

The most effective way I found to run this program was to get a bucket of plastic letters and a card with Yes and a card with No. Put the two cards on the table. Put a plastic letter on the table. Ask, "Is this a 'B'?" Prompt your child to point and say Yes or No appropriately, if needed. As always, end with praise and reinforcement. When he can answer Yes and No appropriately, give him a written prompt to increase the response length. For example, put a B on the table. "Is this a B?" Prompt him, "Yes, that is a B." Put an M on the table. "Is this a P?" "No, that's not a P, that's an M!" Once he can do letters, add other objects. Fade the written cards.

Articulation

Purpose: To improve articulation.

Present your child with written sentences to read. Start with short sentences (e.g., Dog runs.). Also start with words that have sounds that your child can already articulate well. Have him repeat the sentence after you. Make sure he is paying attention to your pronunciation and then looking at the words. It will help him to actually *see* the sounds. As he gets better, add more difficult sounds and longer sentences.

Labeling

Purpose: To increase expressive vocabulary.

Prepare cards with pictures of common people, body parts, food, animals, etc. At first, write the words on the cards together with the pictures. Start with one card on the table at a time. "What is it?" If he does not respond, say it again, and then give him the answer: "Say, 'Ball.'" Ask him again. When he gives the answer, provide praise and reinforcement. When he understands the concept and is complying, and once he is consistently labeling several pictures, take the words off the pictures, and continue the program. Once he understands this program, he may enjoy it immensely. We had stacks of pictures and words that we would flip through with Isaak. There was no "drill and kill." He loved this game! And he learned a tremendous amount of vocabulary.

Simple sentences

Purpose: To form simple sentences.

Prepare sentence strips and accompanying pictures. For example, get pictures of your family members doing different actions: eating, drinking, swinging, etc. Print out short sentences that describe those actions: Mom is eating, Chad is drinking. Cut the sentence strips so that each sentence is separate. Put a picture on the table. Hand your child the sentence strip that accompanies the picture. Prompt him to say the sentence and then match it to the picture. As he understands that concept, add an additional sentence or an additional picture from which to choose. Make it more complex.

Wh– questions

Learning to ask and answer wh– questions will not only increase your child's language abilities, but it may help him become more inquisitive about his environment. Knowledge spurs more interest in gaining more knowledge. The world may begin to open up for him.

Beginning

Purpose: To answer simple, concrete wh– questions.

Prepare common wh– questions that your child should know and their accompanying answers. At first, present one question and one correct answer, and prompt your child to match and read them. As time goes on, make it more complex, adding more answers from which to choose. Make sure you follow up by giving him a chance to answer the questions during the day. Fade the written cues as soon as you can.

Asking why and how

Purpose: To increase spontaneous use of Why and How questions.

Provide your child with an opportunity to ask a question by contriving an appropriate situation. For *why*, place a chair on top of a table, a toy in the bathtub, or a non-food item on a plate. When he notices that something is wrong, he should ask "Why is the toy in the tub?" If he doesn't, give him a written prompt. For *how*, tell him to engage in an action with which he is unfamiliar. For example, tell him to "pretend to be an Alpaca," for which he should ask, "How do I pretend to be an Alpaca?" If he doesn't ask the question independently, give him a written prompt.

Describing how

Purpose: Describe how to complete an activity.

You should have the necessary materials for building, drawing, etc. and a specific object. Your child should be presented with a photo or visual representation of what the object should look like as well as a pre-made recipe, list, or description of the steps. There should be an emphasis on language such as, "First you get _____, next you need _____, then you _____as well as _____ before you get the _____." He should tell you how to make the object. Written prompts should be faded before the picture is faded.

Intraverbals

An intraverbal is more than answering wh– questions. It is responding to what someone else says with something relevant. Intraverbals are gathered from three main sources: features, functions, and class. Learning to identify and use feature, function, and class in your child's language will increase his ability to communicate.

Introduction to feature, function, class

This program will continue for some time. You can introduce it first with simple concepts and targets, and as your child gains more language, you can increase the complexity of the program. Prepare pictures and word cards for the targets. Ask and prompt your child to answer questions related to the feature, function, and class of each target.

- *Feature targets.* Your child should be asked questions such as, "What do you find on a house?" and "Tell me something that has windows."

- *Function targets.* Teach your child to answer a question such as, "What can you cut with?" and "Tell me something that cuts."

- *Class targets.* Your child will be expected to answer a question such as, "What is a tiger?" and "Tell me a kind of animal."

Describing objects (textual and pictorial cues)

Purpose: To accurately describe an object both in and out of view.

Prepare small cards that have description cues on them such as Color, Size, and Function for reference if your child needs help. Ask your child to tell you about an object. He should then be presented with several of those description cards (at least three but no more than five). Try not to ask him a question as you do not want him to depend on questions to talk about objects in his environment. Remember to rotate the description cards that are presented to him so that he does not learn to memorize specific language routines.

Thematic program

Purpose: To provide general intraverbal knowledge about specific themes.

Select a theme around which to organize all of your child's language instruction, e.g., zoo animals. After a theme has been selected, specific targets within the theme should also be selected (specific animals, community helpers, buildings, vehicles, etc.). Remember that the focus of this program is to teach your child to be conversational about multiple topics. There is no pre-determined length for a thematic unit. Units can continue until your child has mastered the majority of the target components. Remember to return to mastered units as well as incorporate a previous unit's targets in new units.

Grammar

Any grammar program can be modified for the child with hyperlexia. Present requests with written cues. Use plastic letters as illustrations. Write out the rules to a certain concept. Use worksheets taken from grammar workbooks. Write down sentences with correct/incorrect grammar and have him identify which is which. Some common grammar concepts to be taught are: possession (it's mine, it's their ball); adverbs (fast/slow, wet/dry); attributes (color, size, shape); prepositions (in/on/under); idioms (bear with me; it's raining cats and dogs).

Verb agreement

Purpose: To understand and use appropriate verb agreement in speech.

Prepare a bunch of sentence strips and accompanying pictures. For example, get pictures of people doing different actions: eating, drinking, swinging, etc. Make sure you have pictures of both singular and plural subjects. Print out short sentences that describe those actions with the helping verb missing:

The girl ____ eating; The boys ____ drinking.

Print *is* and *are* separately. Present your child with the picture, then put the accompanying sentence on the table with the *is/are* choice. Prompt him to put the right helping verb in the space and read it. Once he can do that, put more than one sentence on the table to pick from. Use the same method with other verbs: jump/jumps, run/runs, etc.

Pronouns

Purpose: To understand and use appropriate pronouns.

Use pictures with both familiar people and strangers doing actions. Print out sentences with the full subject (Mom is drinking; The boy is swinging). Also print out pronouns (he, she, they). Present your child with the picture. Give him the full sentence, and have him read it. Prompt him to choose the appropriate pronoun and replace the subject with the pronoun. Have him read it again. Continue making it more complex with different pictures and sentences until he is using pronouns appropriately.

Expressive superlative identification

Purpose: To accurately use superlatives in an expressive manner.

Engage in a turn-taking game where your child is expected to fill in the blanks with the appropriate superlative. For example, if you both have balls and you say, "I have a *big* ball," your child should reply, "My ball is *bigger*" or "I have the *biggest* ball." Present him with visual prompts to begin with, and then fade those visual prompts until he is using superlatives independently.

Expressive identification of irregular plurals

Purpose: To learn to consistently use irregular plurals in everyday speech.

Target at least three specific plurals that will be the focus for a session or a day, e.g., mice, witch, and cat (note that one of these targets is a regular plural). The singular and plural forms of these nouns should be written for your child so that he clearly sees, for example, that one witch = witch, but two witches = witches. Provide your child with numerous opportunities per day to use the target plurals. Keep a running log of the plurals he is learning. This will be his "cheat sheet" to refer to if the need arises. It may be helpful to ask him first to identify *how many* of the specific noun he is talking about, and then teach him to match the number to either the singular or plural form of the noun.

Quantifying verbal responses

Purpose: To use words or phrases to quantify a statement.

This program should be taught in an Expressive Statement–Statement format (you make a statement then have your child make a statement) so that your child hears a quantitative model before he is expected to produce a quantifier on his own. Begin by providing him with the exact language model you expect him to imitate, and, as he progresses, prompt him to generate his own statements.

For example, you may start by taking all the cookies and saying, "I have *all* the cookies," then give all the cookies to your child and prompt him to say, "I have *all* the cookies." After he can do that well, you take all the cookies, and give him all the books. You say, "I have *all* the cookies" and prompt him to say, "I have *all* the books."

Sets: all, some, none, a, the, always, sometimes, never

Adverb game

Purpose: To receptively discriminate between adverbs and the verbs they modify.

This skill should be taught to your child in a game format, either during therapy sessions with an adult or during group sessions with his peers. Adverbs modify verbs and usually end in "ly." Game cards should be prepared from which the players can draw. Cards would initially have a verb such as "run" written on one side and on the other side there should be two adverbs from which your child could choose, e.g., quickly and slowly. When your child draws a card from the pile, he can read the verb and then select one of the adverbs. He will then be asked to demonstrate the verb and adverb, e.g., running quickly.

Expressive identification of "before" and "after"

Purpose: To identify the events of "before" and "after" as related to familiar sequenced events and familiar descriptions of competing specific tasks or projects.

This program should be used only after your child understands and uses the basic concepts of "before" and "after."

Prepare a verbal as well as a textual or pictorial sequence with which your child is familiar, e.g., going to McDonald's, getting dressed, taking a bath. This program is not designed to be a pure sequencing exercise for him but rather to help him identify "before" or "after." You should tell him the story and simultaneously provide him with the textual or pictorial supplementary materials so that he gets a clear visual and auditory understanding of what is being described. When the story is complete, ask him to identify both what happened before and after specific components. Begin with a simple story; "You go to the store. You buy candy. You come home. What happened before you came home?" Use written *before* and *after* cards if he needs them. As your child becomes fluent with this skill, begin fading the extra stimulus cues and make the stories more complex.

Dictionary

Purpose: To expand receptive and expressive vocabulary words.

Prepare worksheets that have the sections Word of the day, Part of speech, Different forms, Definition, and Example on them with blank lines after each. As you come across a word that your child does not know, get out a blank worksheet and fill in the appropriate lines for that word. When you have completed worksheets, you can either keep them in a binder for him to read over, or you can post them on a wall to refer to. It is important to refer back to words that he mastered to keep them fresh in his mind.

Word of the day: ___run___
Part of speech: ___verb___
Different forms: ___I will run; I run;___ ___I am running; I ran___
Definition: ___To go faster than a walk___
Example: ___I can *run* fast___

Social language

Your child can be taught to use social language from the beginning. Teaching him to interact and converse with people will help improve his language skills as well as his social awareness and abilities.

Greetings

Purpose: To receptively and expressively make appropriate greetings.

Prepare "greeting cards" with common greetings written on them such as "Hi!" and "How are you today?" and "See you later." Some cards should have the greeting and then a line for your child to fill in the appropriate name, e.g., "Hi, _____." Set up a situation where he will enter a room and be greeted by you or a peer. Prompt him with the written prompt, if needed, to respond appropriately. Work on appropriate eye contact with this program. Fade the written prompt as soon as possible to help him be independent.

Making contingent statements

Purpose: To make a statement contingent on a previous statement as a means of increasing commenting skills during conversations.

Present your child with a conversation board complete with symbols for various statements that could be made and/or questions that could be asked about a specific topic. Initially, you will introduce a topic of interest, e.g., a new toy in which he is interested. After your comment or question, he should be prompted to refer to his symbol board in order to either answer the question or make a reciprocal comment that is on topic.

If he does not attend to his symbol board, prompt him to point to an appropriate symbol and provide a verbal model, if necessary. If he responds to a comment or question in a non-contingent manner, restate your original comment or question and refer him to at least two symbols from which he could choose that would logically follow. Remember that the goal of this program is to teach him to have conversational exchanges with his partners based on their comments and questions.

Using a computer program called Boardmaker from Mayer-Johnson is a good place to start. These symbols are simple, and most people teaching Picture Exchange Communication System (PECS) use this program. If it is too simple for your child's language level, simply create your own word-, question-, and statement-banks for him to choose from.

Interview

Purpose: To learn to spontaneously ask social questions.

Prepare a worksheet with a variety of social questions such as: what's your name, how old are you, where do you live, what's your favorite food, and what do you like to play? Put the worksheet on a clipboard. Prompt him to ask these questions of different people (whom you have prepared for this). If he can write, have him write down the answers. That will help him pay attention to the answers. If he cannot, you can write the answers for him. After the "interview" is over, go back and ask him, "What did Sally like to play with?" If he cannot remember, take him back to that person to ask again. Mix up the order of the questions each time so that he does not memorize them. Work on eye contact and appropriate body language during this program.

Labeling emotional states associated with verbal responses

Purpose: To use words or phrases to describe emotional states related to a contextual statement.

This program should be done with peers or with props such as puppets. You should provide your child (and his peer if applicable) with a picture or story that targets a specific emotional phrase such as, "I'm sorry" or "I'm happy." Keep the stories brief and the pictures explicit. A sample story would be "Maggie is sad because she cannot have another piece of candy." You should then ask your child what he could say to Maggie. Give him the exact written prompt at first, and as he progresses, encourage more novel responses and fade the written prompts.

Topics

Purpose: To identify what statements are considered on-topic in conversation.

Prepare worksheets with a topic at the top and a list of statements beneath, some of which follow that topic and some of which do not. Have your child read the worksheet and check off which statements pertain to the topic. You will need to change the order of the statements and add new statements regularly so that he does not memorize the answers.

At the beach

- ☐ I found a seashell.
- ☐ I laughed at the zebra.
- ☐ I went down the slide really fast.
- ☐ The giraffe had a long neck.
- ☐ I went up and down on the swing.
- ☐ I used a big umbrella to shade me.
- ☐ I got sand in my shoes.
- ☐ The birds were singing.

At the park

- ☐ I found a seashell.
- ☐ I laughed at the zebra.
- ☐ I went down the slide really fast.
- ☐ I ate my picnic lunch.
- ☐ I went up and down on the swing.
- ☐ The bears were sleeping.
- ☐ I got sand in my shoes.
- ☐ The birds were singing.

Labeling the strength of responses

Purpose: To use words such as "I think, I guess, I know, etc." to describe the certainty of his responses.

Choose a target such as "I think, I guess, I know, I believe, Maybe, etc." and be prepared to provide your child with not only multiple verbal models throughout the day, but also textual cues in situations where it is appropriate for him to make such statements.

You can create opportunities for this program by setting up real life situations, especially in small peer group situations. Engage in an activity such as an art project or taking a walk. You or a peer make statements such as, "I think my bike is really cool" or "I think the sun is really bright today." If your child does not immediately reciprocate with a similar statement (including the target strengthener), then ask him, "What do you think?" Remember that he needs to follow your target model. Provide him with a textual cue for his strengthener.

Non-verbal social cues

Purpose: To increase receptive and expressive non-verbal social cues.

Demonstrate the target non-verbal social cue and ask your child to label it. Next, ask him to identify and use appropriate behaviors in response to that social cue. Also have him demonstrate the target non-verbal cue. Use scripts, verbal explanations, or create worksheets in order to prompt him through this task.

- Shaking head (yes and no)
- Lifting arms (I don't know)
- Shrugging shoulders (oh well)
- Waving hand (come here)
- Pointing (over there/over here)
- Waving hand (no/I don't like that)
- Appropriate facial expression and body language (willing)
- Appropriate facial expression and body language (unwilling)
- Appropriate facial expression and body language (annoyed)

Story telling

Purpose: To tell creative short stories.

Present your child with the opportunity and materials to tell a short story on his own. Initially, model a short story for him. Use a felt board or props when modeling your story. Your child should use the same props when he tells his story. He will be expected to model a story of the same length as yours. It may also be helpful to create a corresponding textual cue to which he can refer while telling the story. Write down his story as he tells it, as it will be reinforcing to him to see it. If he does not begin to tell his story or begins to talk off-topic, refer him back to the felt board or props and provide him with one "jump start" for the next component of the story. This program can be made as simple (1 sentence + The End) or as complex (full story with plot and conclusion) as your child needs to learn.

Chat Bag

Purpose: To make a statement contingent on a previous statement as a means of increasing commenting skills during conversations.

Prepare a special "Chat Bag." The Chat Bag should contain either photos or written topics about which he and another person can have a conversation. Take turns drawing a topic from the bag and initiating the conversation. The goal of this program is to teach your child to engage in conversational exchanges based on his partner's statements. It may be helpful, at least in the original stages of this program, to write or draw each partner's sentences after they are spoken. After the words or pictures are available to him, it will be much easier to direct his attention to specific words and/or concepts in his partner's statements about which he could make a contingent statement or ask a relevant question. This program can be made as simple (an apple or a dog) or as complex (talk about your day at school; talk about your favorite sport) as your child needs to learn. Below is an example of a teaching interaction:

- You pick a picture of a slide out of the Chat Bag.
- You then say, "Some slides are big."
- You write out the sentence.
- If your child does not immediately begin to make a contingent statement, review the written words and verbally model a contingent statement based on one of the words in the statement, e.g. "Yes, the slide at the park is very big."
- Write down his statement.
- After the contingent statement is made, you make another contingent statement based on your child's previous statement.

Re-telling a story

Purpose: To paraphrase a story.

Read or tell your child a story. Immediately after he has heard the story, he should be asked to re-tell it in his own words. He needs to repeat all of the salient details of the story. If you decide that he has missed a detail, he should be re-told or re-read the target amount of story. This program can be made as simple (one sentence) or as complex (three-minute story) as your child needs to learn.

Chapter 10

Theory of Mind

Theory of Mind is the ability to understand that others have thoughts and feelings that are different than one's own. It is the ability to put oneself in someone else's shoes. The lack of this skill is also called mindblindness. Most people with autism spectrum disorders struggle with this ability. In fact, some assert that it is the essence of what autism is—the inability to see from another's perspective and to change one's behavior in accordance with that. The following are some programs that may help your child gain some of those skills.

Picture inferencing

Purpose: To be able to describe what is happening in a picture making appropriate pictorial inferences.

Photocopy some pictures out of children's books of a story which your child does not know. Cut off the words that accompany each picture so that your child is only referring to the picture. Pictures that tell a story and have a lot to imply are the best for this exercise. Present him with a picture and ask him to describe what is happening. If your child needs help, present him with a list of things he could say. At first all the options you offer should all be appropriate, and once he can do that, present him with a list of statements, some of which are appropriate and some which are not. Have him pick which statements to say. Fade the written prompts as soon as you can.

What comes next?

Purpose: To infer a character's actions when presented with a two-dimensional scenario.

Present your child with a picture depicting a scene such as a boy with a baseball and baseball bat. Ask him to identify the salient aspects of the scene, and then ask him to identify what will happen next, e.g., what the boy is going to do. Your child should infer the subsequent actions based only on the information provided in the picture. Refrain from providing him with explicit language models; instead provide him with multiple selections from which he could choose. When he has mastered this program, begin providing him with the opportunity to "predict" what individuals in his environment will do, e.g., follow Mommy around the house and "read" her actions.

"Guess"/"Don't Guess"

Purpose: To make predictions in a story.

Create an index card with "Guess" on one side and "Don't Guess" on the other. Read a short book together. During the story, randomly present your child with either the Guess or Don't Guess side. If Guess is shown, your child should make a prediction about a certain event or detail in the story. If Don't Guess is shown, he should ask a question about the story. If he doesn't respond independently, offer a word/phrase/question bank with options such as "Who is going to ____," "How will they ____," or "He is going to ____."

Verbal inferencing

Purpose: To make more complex inferences in writing and speech.

Read a short book together (without pictures) or give a verbal scenario. After a few sentences or a paragraph, ask him an inferencing question such as, "What do you think he will do?" or "Where do you think they will go?" If he doesn't respond or doesn't know, give him some options from which to choose. It might help to give him a silly answer which he knows is incorrect. "Do you think he will eat an elephant?" That may get him to think about what *might* really happen. Reinforce for correct answers. This program can be made as simple (short paragraph) or as complex (sections from a chapter book) as your child needs to learn.

For the next few Theory of Mind programs, create some figurines and give them names and personalities. These can either be little people or figures that you bought, or you can create them out of cardboard or laminate photographs of familiar people as well as strangers. Describe the familiar people accurately, and give the unfamiliar ones names and unique personalities, e.g., Billy likes tuna sandwiches, running, and playing video games but does not like peas or doing his homework.

Thought bubbles

Purpose: To understand complex private events in other people's minds.

In addition to the figures, you will need a small white board or other means of drawing "thought bubbles."

Step 1

Present your child with one of the figures and a thought bubble. Explain to him that people "get something" like a thought bubble in their heads when they look at other people, objects, and situations. For example, say, "This is Joe. He is looking at a dog. So, Joe gets a thought bubble with a dog in it." Draw a dog in the thought bubble. Next ask him, "What is Joe thinking about?" Present him with multiple thought bubble scenarios (figures looking at objects both including and not including dogs in this example) and ask him to either fill in the figure's thought bubble or tell you what belongs in the bubble.

Step 2

Demonstrate that people can think about things that are not visually present in the moment. Present him with one of the figures (Joe) and a thought bubble. Have Joe look at an object (dog), and fill in the thought bubble. Next, move Joe with the corresponding thought bubble away from the dog until it is in the next room. Ask, "Can Joe see the dog? What is Joe thinking about? What does Joe think is in the next room?"

Step 3

Demonstrate that people's thoughts about the world depend on what they have seen, so if the world changes but a person does not see it change, their thought about the world could stay the same. Present your child with one of the figures (Joe) and a thought bubble. Have Joe look at an object (dog) and fill in the thought bubble, and move Joe with the corresponding thought bubble into the next room. Next, present a second figure. This figure should remove the dog, and replace it with a car. Ask the following questions: "Can Joe see the object? What does Joe think is in the next room? Is he right?"

Step 4

Use the thought bubbles to illustrate predicting other people's actions and private events (such as thoughts). Create a role-playing situation where the figure (Joe) places an object (dog) in a box. Fill in the thought bubble with the dog in a box. Joe should then leave the room. Present the following questions: "Can Joe see the dog? Where does Joe think the dog is? Where will Joe look for the dog?"

Step 5

Illustrate that if someone does not see the location of an object change they will think it is still in the last place where they saw it. Create a role-playing situation similar to the one illustrated in Step 4. This time when Joe leaves the room, a new figure should be introduced. The new figure should remove the dog from the box and place it in another location such as a basket. Present the following questions: "Where is the dog? Where does Joe think the object is? Where will Joe look for the object? Will he be right?"

Step 6

Set up role-playing situations similar to the one illustrated in Step 5. No thought bubbles should be presented for this step. Present the following questions: "Where is the dog? Where does Joe think the dog is? Where will Joe look for the dog? Will he be right?"

Role playing with figures

Purpose: To understand complex private events in other people's minds.

Start this program only after completing the thought bubble program.

Step 1

After your child has reviewed the character descriptions for the figures you will be using in this exercise, a role-play scenario should be set up. For example, "Everybody sits down at the table to eat dinner. They will be eating chicken and carrots." Your child should then be presented with three questions to answer about the perspective of each person.

How would _____ feel based on previous character description?

What would _____ think based on previous character description?

What would _____ do based on previous character description?

Be sure that all questions directly refer to information presented in the personality descriptions. For this step, the answers to the questions will be presented inside thought bubbles above each character as your child should be quite familiar with the thought bubble process. The explicit character descriptions should be visually available. Verbal models and gesture cues to the visual descriptions should be used if he makes an error. For example, if Sally doesn't like carrots, then she would not be happy about dinner tonight.

Step 2

Same as Step 1, but the answers to the questions will no longer be presented inside thought bubbles above each character.

Step 3

Same as Steps 1 and 2, but while the character descriptions will still be visually available, the purpose of this step is to move from exact descriptions of people to more vague descriptions that require some inferencing skills. This step should be broken into three subsets for each scenario, e.g., for the example used above we would move from "Sally does not like carrots" to "Sally does not like vegetables" to "Sally doesn't mind eating vegetables but they are not her favorite."

Step 4

For this step, add past experiences to the characters you will be using (e.g., Joe crashed his bike on the way to school). After your child has reviewed the character descriptions, a role-play scenario should be set up. For example, "After school all of Joe's friends want to go bike riding." The same three questions should be asked about the perspective of each person. The answers to the questions will not be presented inside the thought bubbles. As with the previous step, your child will be required to make some inferences on the part of the character.

Step 5

This step will focus on your child's behavior. A personality description focusing on the character's past experiences (e.g., Joe does not like to play video games) should be assigned to each figure. After your child has reviewed the character descriptions, a role-play scenario should be set up. For example, "Joe comes to your house to play." Your child should then be asked to describe what he and the character would do together, keeping in mind what the character's personality description is. After he has identified what they will do, he should then be presented with the same three questions to answer about the perspective of each person.

Chapter 11

Ten Commandments

Thou shalt see this as a blessing, not a curse

I thought I was pretty optimistic about life. But when I had my first child, the only thing I wanted was for him to be healthy. I agreed with the sentiment that I didn't care what color eyes or hair he had, just that he had ten fingers and ten toes and he was "healthy." Why was that important to me? I really can't answer that question anymore because I now see so many blessings from having a special child. As hard as it has been at times, it is all worth it. I have learned to see *all* people as equal. I have learned not to judge a misbehaving child without knowing the circumstances. I have learned to research and work and fight for my child only to see wonderful things come to fruition. I have learned that financial security is over-rated, and I have no problem giving up all I have to help my child. I have come to appreciate a loving, dedicated husband who is able to step in and be "mom" at a moment's notice. I have seen a little sister who sees a child with a disability no differently than a typical child because she has been involved with them every day of her life. There is no end to the blessings our family have received, and they well outweigh the challenges we have had to endure.

Thou shalt accept help

Realize that there is no way that you can do this alone. It is hoped you have a supportive family. Let your partner be a part of your child's therapy and education. The fact is that you're going to need a break once in a while, and if you don't have someone who can step in when needed, you're not going to get that respite. When people offer help, take it. When your life gets easier, make sure you give back. When you can, offer help to others that could use help. Pay it forward!

Thou shalt be proactive

Whether it is with school, with a professional, or with a situation in the community, there will be times that you will need to step forward and assert yourself on behalf of your child. Your child depends on you to do so. You are his voice and advocate. No one loves him like you do. No one will protect him like you. You will need to be proactive. Sitting back and waiting for him to "grow out of it" may do nothing but postpone the grief. Get over it now. Realize he needs help, and press forward with clarity.

Thou shalt be educated and educate others

I know in the beginning it seems like an insurmountable task. There is so much to learn, so much research and reading, to even get a small grip on it. And it seems like the more you learn, the more you have to learn; and the more progress your child makes, the further it may seem he has to go. The only way I felt I had a handle on it was to be constantly educated. The more information I had, the better I was able to serve my son. In turn, you need to take the information you gain and give it to others. Educate school personnel and professionals about hyperlexia. Get the word out there and pave the path for other parents who come after you. Remember how hard it was for you in the beginning without that "user's guide" to direct you. Provide the information you have learned to others who are struggling.

Thou shalt not agree to something you feel is not in the best interest of your child

Through your research and your innate sense of who your child is, you will have the best ability to know what is best for your child. Although the professionals you have may know your child's disorder better than you, you know your child better than anyone. You are the expert on your child. Couple your solid research with your instincts to pursue the help you feel is right for him. You have no reason to agree to anything that goes against those instincts. You have those instincts for a reason. Look at a situation from a different angle. Get a second, third, even fourth opinion. When it's right, you'll feel it, then you can go forward with the ardor you need.

Thou shalt not disregard his gifts

Do not let anyone tell you these are "just" splinter skills and not functional. They may be splinter skills, true, but they *are* useful. Take advantage of the wonderful gift your child has been given. Foster the love for the written word. Teach him through his talents. Teach him how to *use* those talents. Embrace who he is.

Thou shalt be patient

I know you want everything to be better right now, but progress takes time. It will be frustrating. There will be days when you can't imagine him ever calling your name, ever holding a conversation, ever being sociable. Your child's own potential will emerge, but it may take time. Expect fallbacks. The process is often two steps forward and one step back. Just as soon as you have mastered one skill, another problem may creep in. Remember that going two forward and one back is *still* going forward. Sometimes it helps to look back to see how far you've come. Those early years are so hard. They will pass. Things will get better.

Thou shalt network with other parents

This is so important. You need to meet other parents who are struggling, too. You can pool resources, get information, bounce ideas off each other, and know that you are not alone in this. I know a best friend is important, but even your best friend cannot fully comprehend what it's like to have a child with challenges. That friend will try to empathize and may say, "Oh, I have the same problem with my child" in the hopes that you don't feel alone. But it will only be another parent with a special child that can truly understand those deep, significant feelings. You will need that connection.

Thou shalt not ignore your other children or spouse

This will be hard at times. You will feel like you have to address this urgent issue with your special child, and your family just has to wait. In a way, that's true. Your family will learn some important lessons such as charity and love because of your special child. But do not take them for granted. Remember that, to them, life may seem like it revolves around your special child. *The New York Times* recently published an article about siblings. Don Meyer put it well in that article. "There's bound to be resentment when the emotional and financial resources are all wrapped up in one kid. It's Johnny this, Johnny that, the United States of Johnny. Johnny is the sun in the family's solar system" (Gross 2004). Although you certainly love *all* your children, you need to make a special effort that they all *feel* it. That means taking special time to spend with your other children, one-on-one. It means making each child feel accomplished and important. It means setting time aside for you and your husband. It means making sure the marriage doesn't crumble under the pressure of this challenge. Having a stable home environment will help your child feel safe and secure.

Thou shalt love your child with all your heart, might, mind, and strength

It all comes down to that. If you love your child, you will do what you can to help him. With love in your heart, you will be able to survive those difficult days. You not only know your child, but you have an innate sense of truth when it comes to his needs. No one is more important to your child and his well-being than you. You are his world. And he is yours. And with that, there is nothing more rewarding in life. Nothing equals the love of a parent for a child.

Special Education Law in the United States

Special education law terms

504 Plan   This refers to Section 504 of the 1973 Rehabilitation Act. It means that a student with a documented disability, who does not qualify for full special education services, can still receive accommodations that will ensure he gets an appropriate and fair education. A 504 Plan only allows for accommodations and modifications with no goals and no right to special services. It's the difference between only *accommodations* and full *services*.

FAPE   Free Appropriate Public Education. Legal term under IDEA which states that a child with a disability is entitled to an appropriate education, according to his needs, at public expense.

Goals and Objectives   Annual goals are created by the IEP team in direct relationship to the PLOPs. Goals may be academic, address social or behavioral needs, relate to physical needs, or address other educational needs. Goals must be clear and measurable.

IDEA   Individuals with Disabilities Education Act. Special education law in the United States that mandates that a child with a disability gets a Free Appropriate Public Education. The Act lays out clearly what that means.

IEE   Independent Educational Evaluation. An outside evaluation done at public expense if a parent disagrees with an evaluation obtained by the school district.

IEP   Individualized Education Program. The written plan devised by school and home personnel with specifics on how the individual child (aged three to adult) will be educated. Typically the IEP team consists of you as a parent or legal guardian, a special education teacher, a general education teacher (if the child will be participating in general education), and a representative from the local educational agency (LEA) who has knowledge about special education (generally a school administrator). Other possible members of the team may be your own professionals, other knowledgeable persons not affiliated with the school, the child (if able), a special education advocate, or other school district personnel.

IFSP Individualized Family Service Plan. The written plan devised by school and home personnel with specifics on how the individual child (aged birth to three) will be educated.

LEA Local Education Agency. The public authority (e.g., board of education; school district administrators) within a state which maintains administrative control of public schools.

LRE Least-Restrictive Environment. Legal term under IDEA which states that a child with a disability is entitled to be educated with his typical peers to the maximum extent appropriate. Special classes, separate schooling, or other removal of children with disabilities from the regular educational environment should occur only when the severity of the disability is such that education in regular classes with the use of supplementary aids and services *cannot* be achieved satisfactorily.

PLOP Present Levels of Performance. Descriptive statements in the IEP of how the child is performing in specific areas of need according to evaluations, including strengths, interests, and needs. This is where the strengths of a child with hyperlexia can be highlighted.

SDI Specially Designed Instruction. How instruction will be adapted or modified to help the student meet the annual goal, e.g., written instructions when oral instructions are given to other students; student checklist of daily expectations; reinforcement schedule.

The special education process
Step 1

If your child is under three years old, call the school district and have them refer you to their birth to three program. This program is called something different in each state, and each school district runs the program a little differently. The birth to three age range is not as clearly dictated under IDEA; however, services are still required to be offered.

Step 2

If your child is at least three years old, call the school district and tell them that you need to get your child evaluated for special education services. You may only need to make the call, but depending on how responsible your school district is, you may also need to present the request in writing. Do so to the school district office. Parental consent is needed before the child may be evaluated. Your school district will send you a form to sign to have the process started. Evaluation needs to be completed within a reasonable time after you give consent.

Step 3

Get the evaluations done. These need to assess your child globally, even if you do not suspect problems in one area. You need to have an overall picture of your child's strengths and weaknesses. This will likely include a speech and language assessment, occupational and physical evaluations, a behavioral assessment, assessment of social skills, and possibly achievement or intelligence testing. You may choose to have private testing and evaluations done in addition to what the school is doing. I recommend you do this, if for nothing more than a second opinion. You cannot be sure if you will need that private documentation. If you have respectable insurance, just get the evaluations done on your own. You may choose to keep your child in private therapy anyway. If you do not have good insurance, you can ask for an Independent Educational Evaluation (IEE). You can ask that the school system pay for this IEE, but generally you have to have a good reason to get it granted. I reiterate—get a private evaluation done on your own if you are able.

Step 4

You should sit down with your school personnel after all the evaluations have been completed. You will look at and discuss all the results. Ask all your questions here. Get as much information as you can as early as possible. You don't know at this point what information you will need and what you will not. Your school district will let you know of their determinations. If your child has a documented disability but only requires accommodations, a 504 Plan may be created. If he fits the IDEA profile for special education, then an IEP will be created. If it is determined that he neither has a disability nor needs special education, services will not be offered. If you disagree with your school's decision, you have the right to ask for a hearing to challenge that decision.

Step 5

If your child is found eligible for services, a team will be assembled to create an IEP. School personnel must let you know in writing when the IEP meeting is scheduled and do so far enough in advance so that you can make arrangements to attend. They must also try to make it at a time and place that is convenient for you. They should let you know that you can bring anyone who knows or works with your child to help create a constructive document. You may record the IEP meeting with permission, but I suggest you only do this if you have an irrefutable reason. It generally makes your school personnel nervous and defensive, and you do want to have good relations with them. The IEP cannot be completed before the actual IEP meeting takes place. Once the IEP is created and goals are written and placement decided on, you have to give written consent for it to be implemented. If you disagree with the contents of the IEP, try to work it out with your team first. If there is no way to come to an agreement after several meetings, and you still feel your child will not be served appropriately, you can ask for mediation where an objective mediator will come and help resolve issues between you and the school. This is at the school's expense. If you still cannot come to an agreement, then you are entitled to pursue due process. This is a legal proceeding much like a court case. A hearing officer will hear the case and make a decision. If none of that needs to happen and you agree with the school findings and the IEP, then once it's signed and you have your copy, your child should begin services immediately.

Step 6

You should be in regular contact with your school personnel. You may find at this time that your point-of-contact is your child's teacher. You should receive regular reports on progress and problems. You should also receive official reports at least as often as the typical student does. It is to be hoped that is not the only time you are receiving reports, though. Stay in contact with your teachers and staff. Keep a good relationship. Note any changes at home and let the school know. What has worked best for us in the past is a "Communication Notebook." It's a notebook that goes back and forth to school in my son's backpack where I write notes to the teacher or aide and they write back. It could be anything from "He woke up too early this morning and is a bit crabby" to "He had a wonderful recess and played with two new friends!"

Step 7

The IEP needs to be reviewed at least annually. However, I have always had to call for a bi-annual meeting because Isaak's development changes so rapidly. Even though we create goals we think might last a year, he seems to exceed our expectations every time. Sometimes the IEP just needs a new amendment, but sometimes we have to write a new one. You might think that he's mastering all the available goals since he progresses so fast, but as he gets older and the social expectations continue to increase, we find we still have a lot of work to do. At any time, you can disagree with an IEP. You sign it and indicate "disagree" right on the IEP, in which case the school district needs to indicate in writing what the disagreement was and what will be done to work out a resolution. At least every three years, your child will be reevaluated to see if he still qualifies as a child with a disability as dictated by IDEA.

Legal documentation

In the United States, IDEA is the most recent law that governs the application of special education. The law is long and detailed, and many of those details will be irrelevant to your situation. Much of the law is about funding and the logistics of who reports to whom. There is a lot of financial information in the law and committee make-up. Some of the law you will recognize either from your own research or from what your school has communicated to you. Some of it may not be information your school is eager to give you or perhaps information they even know. What follows is a list of information in the law that has been useful to know for other parents of children with hyperlexia and autism and related disorders. This is not an inclusive list of everything that might be important to your situation, but it has some of the most popular need-to-know information, and it is a good place to start. The entire law is readily available on the web. Keep in mind that your state can lose their funding from the federal government if they do not follow this law with exactness, so it is beneficial to you to know what the requirements are and to help your school district adhere to those requirements.

You can read the actual law on the Internet (One Hundred Fifth Congress of the United States of America 1997). Here is some of what you will find in IDEA.

Evaluations, assessments, diagnosis, and placement

- Autism is specifically mentioned as a qualification under "child with a disability" [602(3)(A)(i)].

- A child without an autism diagnosis may still qualify for services per diagnostic testing [602(3)(B)(i)].

- A parent's consent is required in writing before any evaluations are conducted [614(a)(1)(C)(i) and 614(b)(1)]; however, if the school can prove that they tried to get consent but were unable to get the parent to respond, they can go ahead with evaluations and placements [614(c)(3)].

- A child shall be reevaluated for special education placement and services whenever it's deemed prudent or whenever a parent or teacher requests it, but at least every three years [614(a)(2)(A)].

- A variety of assessment tools and information are required to complete the evaluation of a child [614(b)(2)].

- Evaluation materials must be presented in a child's native tongue or other mode of communication [614(b)(3)(A)(ii)]. This might be useful in requesting that evaluations be done in written form for a child with hyperlexia, although I have not seen that pursued.

- Standardized tests and evaluations must be administered by trained personnel [614(b)(3)(B)(ii)].

- Evaluations need to be comprehensive [614(b)(3)(D)].

- A parent must be involved in the determination of disability status for the child. The parent must be given copies of the evaluations and determinations [614(b)(4)].

- Educational personnel are required to review any additional documentation provided by the parent, including private evaluation reports, in making any educational placement and services decisions [614(c)(1)(A)].

- The child's strengths have to be taken into consideration [614(d)(3)(A)].

- Parents must be involved in the placement decisions of their child [614(f)].

- Parents are entitled to review all educational records on their child [615(b)(1)].

- Parents must be notified in writing prior to any changes in their child's placement or services [615(b)(3)]. Notification must include why they are making changes and what other options were considered and rejected [615(c)].

Services

- Free and Appropriate Public Education (FAPE) means just that—free and appropriate—at no cost to you and in accordance with a signed (by you) Individual Education Plan (IEP) [602(8)].

- Special equipment deemed necessary for the child's learning can be purchased with educational funds [605(a)].

- A child is still entitled to services in accordance with the IEP even if he has been suspended or expelled [612(a)(1)(A)].

- Educational services must be provided in a timely manner [612(a)(2)].

- A child is entitled to an education in a Least Restrictive Environment (LRE). This should be an education "to the maximum extent appropriate" with his typically-developing peers with appropriate support [612(a)(5)(A)].

- A child attending (for whatever reason) a non-public school can still receive services through the public school system in accordance with the IEP. Such services can be provided at the non-public school [612(a)(10)(A)(i)(II)].

- Special education students are entitled to special accommodations when taking standardized tests [612(a)(17)].

- A local school is authorized to join with another local school to provide for the needs of your child if they cannot meet the needs themselves [613(e)(1)(A)].

- The state educational agency can take over the funds and provide services for your child if it determines that the local public school is not complying with all the standards and the law [613(h)].

- Positive behavior plans must be put in place to address behavior problems [614(d)(3)(B)(i)].

Training

- A paraprofessional or aide to your child must be appropriately trained and supervised [612(a)(15)(B)(iii)].

- Educational personnel should make "an ongoing good-faith effort to recruit and hire appropriately and adequately trained personnel" to work with your child [612(a)(15)(C)].

- A local school is authorized to reevaluate how their system is working in regards to all the children on IEPs every three years. Parents should be on the committee that makes that determination, must actually show agreement in writing, and be involved in the carrying out of the decisions made in that committee. Such decisions shall be made known to the greater parent community [613(g)(4) and 613(g)(6)].

IEP

- The IEP must contain: the child's present level of performance; annual and short-term goals; what supports the child needs (e.g., aide time, special break time, behavior management system); how much the child will *not* participate with typical children; level of participation in standardized tests with typical children; dates for beginning of services and frequency of such and how goals will be measured; transition services needed to help the child into adulthood; parental notification of progress [614(d)(1)(A)].

- A parent is part of the IEP team, together with the special education and regular education teachers and appropriate school professional personnel. Additional personnel can be part of the team if deemed necessary, including the child [614(d)(1)(B)].

- An IEP should be in place for each child at the beginning of each school year. An IFSP (Individualized Family Service Plan) is sufficient for a child turning three during the school year if it meets the guidelines and is agreed to by the parents [614(d)(2)].

- The IEP should be reviewed and modified *at least* once a year [614(d)(4)(A)(i)].

Conflict resolution

- The school is required to document disciplinary actions against the child and include that documentation in his permanent record [613(j)].

- Educational personnel have to provide a way for a parent to file an official complaint regarding their child's placement or services [615(b)(6)].

- A parent or the school is entitled to call for mediation as a mechanism for conflict resolution. Mediation is voluntary and cannot be used to deny or delay a parent's right to further legal action. The mediator must be qualified and *impartial*. The State has to pay for all mediation costs. Mediation sessions must be scheduled in a timely manner and convenient to the parties involved. Any decisions made in mediation must be put in writing; however, discussions during mediation are confidential [615(e)].

- A parent or the school is entitled to call for a due process hearing if all other avenues to resolve a conflict have failed. This is a legal proceeding. Documentation to be used on both sides must be shared before the hearing [615(f)].

- A due process hearing decision can be appealed [615(g)].

- Some attorney fees may be covered if the parent wins a case in due process [615(i)(3)(B)].

- A child has to remain in the current educational setting during any legal proceedings until the process is complete [615(j)].

- A child can be disciplined (such as suspension) for similar reasons to typical children, but a behavior plan has to be created or modified after such action [615(k)(1)].

- Educational personnel can pull a child unilaterally from a placement if they determine that the child is dangerous to self or others. However, they do have to prove such a decision, and the parent has an opportunity to appeal [615(k)].

The young child

- Infants and toddlers up to age three are entitled to services according to the State [631(b)].

- Services to infants and toddlers are provided at home and/or in community locations [632(4)(G)].

- Infants and toddlers qualify for services if their development delayed in at least one area, have a qualifying diagnosis, or, according to the State's policies, are simply at risk [632(5)].

- IFSP is to be evaluated at least once a year with reviews with the parents at least every six months [636(b)].

- Services may begin before the final assessments and IFSP are complete [636(c)].

- Meetings to begin the transition process into preschool shall begin *at least* 90 days before the child turns three [637(a)(8)(A)(ii)(II)].

Here are a few things you won't find in IDEA.

Evaluations, assessments, diagnosis, and placement

- Educational personnel are *not* authorized to make a medical diagnosis—only to develop, manage, and provide services [602(4)(A)(i)].

- Educational personnel cannot make a placement determined upon only one evaluation or recommendation: "no single procedure shall be the sole criterion for determining an appropriate educational program for a child" [612(a)(6)(B) and 614(b)(2)].

- Educational personnel cannot deny services or postpone placement past the third birthday if an IEP has been agreed upon (for example, if there is no room in a classroom or a specialist hasn't been hired yet) [612(a)(9)].

- Parental consent for evaluation cannot be construed as parental consent for placement [614(a)(1)(C)(i)].

- A reevaluation does not have to be postponed until the three-year mark, but can take place at any time it is requested [614(a)(2)(A)].

- Educational personnel cannot unilaterally determine that a child no longer qualifies for services without going through the proper channels (getting parental approval, giving the appropriate evaluations, etc.) [614(c)(5)].

- A child does not need to prove a major developmental delay to get services. I've heard that they have to show a two standard deviation delay in two areas. It's not in the Law. It may be a State decision, but it is not in the Federal law [602(3) and 632(5)].

Services

- Educational personnel cannot deny services or supplementary aids on the basis that they will be used by typical children as well as the special education child [613(a)(4)(A)].

Rules and regulations

- Educational personnel are *not* authorized to create new regulations and require adherence to such regulations that are not specific in IDEA without following the official US Code for making new rules [607(c)]. They can't make up their own rules.

- Special education funds appropriated to your child cannot be used in the general education fund for other purposes. The money allocated to your child is for that use alone [612(a)(18)(B)].

Conflict resolution

- Educational personnel are not required to pay for a non-public school placement if a Free and Appropriate Public Education was offered (deciding what is considered "appropriate" is the question that may require legal intervention). However, they are required to reimburse parents for such a private placement if it is determined by a court that the public school did not provide an appropriate education in a timely manner [612(a)(10)(C)]. Be cautious, though: there are stipulations that need to be considered such as giving notice to the public school of an upcoming withdrawal.

Some Useful Organizations in the UK

The National Autistic Society
393 City Road
London EC1V 1NG
Website: www.autism.org.uk
Autism helpline: 0845 070 4004
Advocacy for Education Service: 0845 070 4002

The Children's Legal Centre
University of Essex
Wivenhoe Park
Colchester CO4 3FQ
Tel: 0845 120 2966 (open 10.00 am–1.00 pm)
An independent national charity operating an Education Law and Advocacy Unit. Solicitors and barristers provide free legal advice on all aspects of education law.

Contact a Family
209–211 City Road
London EC1V 1JN
Freephone helpline: 0808 808 3555
E-mail: info@cafamily.org.uk
Website: www.cafamily.org.uk
A national support group for the families of those with special needs.

Education Otherwise
PO Box 7420
London N9 9SG
Tel: 0870 765 3510 (England), 0870 765 3580 (Scotland), 0870 765 3610 (Ireland), 0870 765 3620 (Wales)
Website: www.education-otherwise.org
A membership organization you should contact if you want to home-school your child, offering support and information.

OAASIS (Office for Advice, Assistance, Support and Information on Special Needs)
Brock House
Grigg Lane
Brockenhurst
Hampshire SO47 7RE
Tel: 09068 633201
Website: www.oaasis.co.uk
Offers useful leaflets and advice for people going through the "system."

Appendix C

Glossary and Diagnostic Criteria

Glossary

ABA   Applied Behavior Analysis. A systematic and individualized program that breaks down skills into small parts, and builds upon them incrementally to teach a child important life skills.

ABLLS   *The Assessment of Basic Language and Learning Skills.* This is a book by James W. Partington and Mark L. Sundberg (1998) and is an assessment, curriculum guide, and skills tracking system for children with language delays. It contains a task analysis of skills necessary to communicate successfully and be able to learn from everyday experiences.

antecedent   Situation that influences behavior. What happens *before* a behavior occurs.

AVB   Applied Verbal Behavior. Focuses on teaching specific components of expressive language first such as mands (requests for wants and needs), tacts (labeling or describing objects), and intraverbals (verbal responses under control of other verbal behavior).

behavior modification (b-mod)   To extinguish an undesirable behavior (by removing the reinforcer) and replace it with a desirable behavior by reinforcement.

BIP   Behavior Intervention Plan. A behavior plan developed from information obtained after an FBA; should include positive strategies, programs or curricular modifications, and supplementary aids and supports required to address the behaviors of concern.

chaining   Breaking down a skill into small units and teaching each separately and linking each unit to the next until the entire skill is mastered.

chunking Taking a phrase previously learned or heard and using it as a whole at another time to convey meaning, e.g., "What would you like for dinner?" *"I'm having fish tonight!"* from the movie, *Finding Nemo.*

DIR Developmental, Individual Differences, Relationship. Approach developed by Dr. Stanley Greenspan which focuses on the emotional development of the child. The goal of the treatment is to help the child master the healthy emotional milestones that were missed in his early development and which are critical to learning.

DTT Discrete Trial Training. One facet of an ABA program. It is an instruction cycle, repeated several times in succession or over time until a skill is mastered. The parts include discriminative stimulus (S^D) (instruction or cue), prompting stimulus (S^P) (optional prompt), response (R) (from child), reinforcing stimulus (S^R) (reward given to encourage the correct response again), and inter-trial interval (^{ITI}) (pause between trials).

echolalia The repetition of words instead of reciprocating language, e.g., "Do you want a cookie?" *"Want a cookie?"*

extinction The discouragement of a behavior that used to be reinforced by no longer reinforcing it (essentially the ignoring of a behavior).

fading Gradually prompting less and less so as to help the child become more independent in the task; reducing the number of times a reinforcement is given or the type of reinforcement so that eventually the only reinforcement is intrinsic in the task.

FBA Functional Behavior Assessment. The process of determining the cause (or "function") of a behavior before developing an intervention. It should include an antecedent (what happens before the behavior), description of the behavior, and a consequence (what happens after the behavior).

Floortime Usually incorporated with DIR. An approach that involves meeting a child at his current developmental level, and building upon his particular set of strengths; typically an adult waits for the child to express interest in a particular skill, and then helps him build upon that interest.

learned helplessness Child believes he is not capable of doing something because someone else is always doing it for him.

prompt   Presenting something to the child that will assist the child in producing the correct response. Examples of prompts are verbal (instruction or cue), modeling (showing the child what to do), physical (hand-over-hand assisting), gestural (pointing or indicating), and positional (arranging materials in such a way as to increase the likelihood of a correct response).

prompt dependence   Child waits for prompting to occur even though he may have the ability to complete the task without prompting.

PRT   Pivotal Response Training Theory. An intervention developed by Robert Koegel and Laura Schreibman based on the principles of ABA; works to increase motivation by including components such as child choice, turn-taking, reinforcing attempts, and interspersing maintenance tasks.

RDI   Relationship Development Intervention. This was developed by Dr. Steven Gutstein and teaches social interactions on a deeper level than "scripts" using familiar points of reference and inference.

reinforcer   Something given that will increase the likelihood of a behavior occurring again, e.g., candy given after a correct response (if the child likes candy, it will increase the likelihood that he'll give the correct response again) or giving a child a toy that he is screaming for (will increase the likelihood of screaming occurring the next time).

schedules of reinforcement   Only some instances of the desired response are reinforced. This is a way to increase independence of a task or response.

shaping   Reinforcing a behavior that in any way resembles the desired behavior, then reinforcing behavior closer to the desired behavior, and so on until the child is performing the desired behavior independently.

splinter skills   A set of skills that are far above what would be expected in relation to intellectual age, e.g., an eight-year-old who can't write his name but can play the piano beautifully or a three-year-old who can't carry on a conversation but can read chapter books.

TEACCH   Treatment and Education of Autistic and related Communication handicapped CHildren. An individualized assessment and treatment program developed at the University of North Carolina for children with autism and developmental disabilities. It includes a focus on the child with autism and the development of a program around a child's skills, interests, and needs. Self-contained autism classrooms often use this approach.

token economy   Giving reinforcement after a fixed number of correct responses. Correct responses are noted by "tokens," e.g., after ten stickers (given by correct responses), a ten-minute break is given.

Diagnostic criteria
299.00 Autistic Disorder

(A)   A total of six (or more) items from (1), (2), and (3), with at least two from (1), and one each from (2) and (3):

   (1)   qualitative impairment in social interaction, as manifested by at least two of the following:

      (a)   marked impairment in the use of multiple nonverbal behaviors such as eye-to-eye gaze, facial expression, body postures, and gestures to regulate social interaction

      (b)   failure to develop peer relationships appropriate to developmental level

      (c)   a lack of spontaneous seeking to share enjoyment, interests, or achievements with other people (e.g., by a lack of showing, bringing, or pointing out objects of interest)

      (d)   lack of social or emotional reciprocity

   (2)   qualitative impairments in communication as manifested by at least one of the following:

      (a)   delay in, or total lack of, the development of spoken language (not accompanied by an attempt to compensate through alternative modes of communication such as gestures or mime)

      (b)   in individuals with adequate speech, marked impairment in the ability to initiate or sustain a conversation with others

      (c)   stereotyped and repetitive use of language or idiosyncratic language

      (d)   lack of varied, spontaneous make-believe play or social imitative play appropriate to developmental level

   (3)   restricted repetitive and stereotyped patterns of behavior, interests, and activities, as manifested by at least one of the following:

(a) encompassing preoccupation with one or more stereotyped patterns of interest that is abnormal either in intensity or focus

(b) apparently inflexible adherence to specific, nonfunctional routines or rituals

(c) stereotyped and repetitive motor mannerisms (e.g., hand or finger flapping or twisting, or complex whole-body movements)

(d) persistent preoccupation with parts of objects.

(B) Delays or abnormal functioning in at least one of the following areas, with onset prior to the age three years:

(1) social interaction

(2) language as used in social communication, or

(3) symbolic or imaginative play.

(C) The disturbance is not better accounted for by Rett's Disorder or Childhood Disintegrative Disorder.

(*DSM-IV* 1994)

299.80 Asperger's Disorder

(A) Qualitative impairment in social interaction, as manifested by at least two of the following:

(1) marked impairment in the use of multiple nonverbal behaviors such as eye-to-eye gaze, facial expression, body postures, and gestures to regulate social interaction

(2) failure to develop peer relationships appropriate to developmental level

(3) a lack of spontaneous seeking to share enjoyment, interests, or achievements with other people (e.g., by a lack of showing, bringing, or pointing out objects of interest to other people)

(4) lack of social or emotional reciprocity.

(B) Restricted repetitive and stereotyped patterns of behavior, interests, and activities, as manifested by at least one of the following:

(1) encompassing preoccupation with one or more stereotyped and restricted patterns of interest that is abnormal either in intensity or focus

(2)   apparently inflexible adherence to specific, non-functional routines or rituals

(3)   stereotyped and repetitive motor mannerisms (e.g., hand or finger flapping or twisting, or complex whole-body movements)

(4)   persistent preoccupation with parts of objects.

(C)   The disturbance causes clinically significant impairment in social, occupational, or other important areas of functioning.

(D)   There is no clinically significant general delay in language (e.g., single words used by age two, communicative phrases used by age three).

(E)   There is no clinically significant delay in cognitive development or in the development of age-appropriate self-help skills, adaptive behavior (other than in social interaction), and curiosity about the environment in childhood.

(F)   Criteria are not met for another specific Pervasive Developmental Disorder or Schizophrenia.

(*DSM-IV* 1994)

Pervasive Developmental Disorder Not Otherwise Specified (including atypical autism)

This category should be used when there is a severe and pervasive impairment in the development of reciprocal social interaction or verbal and nonverbal communication skills, or when stereotyped behavior, interests, and activities are present, but the criteria are not met for a specific Pervasive Developmental Disorder, Schizophrenia, Schizotypal Personality Disorder, or Avoidant Personality Disorder. For example, this category includes "atypical autism"—presentations that do not meet the criteria for Autistic Disorder because of late age of onset, atypical symptomatology, or subthreshold symptomatology, or all of these.

Other disorders
AD(H)D

Attention Deficit (Hyperactivity) Disorder affects one's ability to maintain attention, control impulsivity, and hyperactivity. Children may appear flighty, not able to sit still or complete a task, and they act impulsively, not appearing to understand nor care about the consequences of their actions. They may appear oblivious to society's norms of social expectations. They may act ego-centrically—only taking into account the impact of something on themselves. AD(H)D is not a result of a growth spurt or a difficult life situation. It is chronic and pervasive. The symptoms do not come and go. They persist throughout all environments, even if seen in different forms.

Having AD(H)D can affect children's ability to communicate. They may blurt out answers. Their thought processes may seem disorganized. They may not listen to the other speaker and, as a result, may return information that is irrelevant.

Apraxia

Apraxia is a nervous system disorder that affects a child's ability to process and produce sounds. It affects a child's oral motor abilities. Children may not babble as much as other children, and their first words may be later. Their pronunciation may be significantly impaired. They may not be able to make certain sounds, and the same word may sound different at various times. They may seem to be groping to create a sound. Receptive language is not usually affected. All of these symptoms go well beyond what is developmentally expected.

Central Auditory Processing Disorder

An audiologist usually renders this diagnosis after specialized testing. The testing is generally not reliable until the child is older. The disorder has to do with the ability to process auditory sounds and manage the information correctly. These children have problems localizing where sound is coming from, distinguishing one sound from another, determining patterns of sounds, sequencing sounds, being able to filter out background noise when trying to gather information, and having the ability to understand when information is missing. These children have problems with listening comprehension, following oral directions, and short-term auditory memory. They usually have early language delays. They may have problems learning words to songs, or they may seem overly sensitive to loud surroundings like a birthday party. Children with CAPD often struggle learning to read because they cannot hear the sounds correctly. They often learn coping strategies like learning to read body language as they get older. CAPD is sometimes mistaken for ADHD or high-functioning autism, but children with CAPD generally do not have the same problems if the learning environment is altered, whereas ADHD and HFA symptoms are pervasive.

Learning Disabled

A learning disability is an unexpected discrepancy between potential and actual achievement. These children have difficulty in one or more of the following areas: listening, speaking, reading, written expression, mathematics, and reasoning.

Some common disorders identified among children with hyperlexia are an articulation disorder, an expressive language disorder (what the child can speak), a receptive language disorder (what the child can understand), a motor skills disorder, or simply a developmental disorder that doesn't fit any other category.

Nonverbal Language Disorder

NLD (or NVLD) children are extremely bright. They are frequently identified as gifted from an early age due to their high verbal abilities. They often read early, but their comprehension may lag behind. They may have trouble socializing and be physically awkward. They have more problems as they get older and academics become more abstract and social situations more complex. They have trouble organizing and can be inattentive. Their pragmatic language may be impaired. NLD children may struggle with math, handwriting, and organizational skills. NLD often mimics Asperger Syndrome, and only a qualified professional can give an appropriate diagnosis. You would probably be more likely to get an NLD diagnosis from a speech therapist and an Asperger Syndrome diagnosis from a medical doctor.

Semantic-Pragmatic Language Disorder

Semantic-Pragmatic language disorder, or SPD, is similar to NLD except that language is more impaired. It is perhaps more closely related to high-functioning autism than Asperger Syndrome. Whereas a child with Asperger Syndrome may have more social problems than a child with SPD, the child with SPD has more early language difficulties. Young children with SPD may respond to sounds, but often ignore their own name. Often their language skills do develop, and they usually develop coping strategies by about age four. By school age, they are differentiated more when they are not socializing like their peers, and they have problems with the pragmatics of language. Many children with SPD learn language by chunking or by echolalia. Children with SPD are detail thinkers—picking out the specifics of something instead of grasping the whole of the subject. They require sameness and routine to function well. They do not have the same problem with math, handwriting, organization, or attention that children with NLD do. Because they have problems processing language, they are easily distracted by the noise of a classroom or similar situation. By school age, they test reasonably well on language tests because the tests are very concrete, and as such, the difficulties these children experience may be ignored, or the child may be labeled as having behavior problems. It is more likely that they are not processing information and language correctly. As they mature and language requirements become more abstract, their deficits become more obvious.

Sensory Integration Disorder

Sensory integration is the method our brain goes through to process all the information it receives through the senses. Most of us do this without effort or awareness, but for some children, some of the senses are hyper- (over) or hypo- (under) stimulated. Children may be over-sensitive to sounds or under-sensitive to touch or any of a number of imbalances. With the brain processing input so erratically and being overwhelmed by too much or too little information, learning difficulties arise. Language is often impaired, physical coordination is affected, and it can cause problems that run the gamut of a child's development.

References

American Hyperlexia Association (AHA) (2003) *What Is Hyperlexia?* Retrieved December 14, 2004 from http://www.hyperlexia.org/aha_what_is.html.

American Psychiatric Association (1994) *Diagnostic and Statistical Manual of Mental Disorders*, 4th edition. Washington, DC: American Psychiatric Association.

Burd, L. and Kerbeshian, J. (1985) 'Hyperlexia and a Variant of Hypergraphia.' *Perceptual and Motor Skills 50*, 940–942.

Bush, G. (1990) *Remarks of President George Bush at the Signing of the Americans with Disabilities Act.* Retrieved December 2, 2004 from http://www.eeoc.gov/abouteeoc/35th/videos/ada_signing_text.html.

Charlop-Christy, M.H. and Haymes, L.K. (1998) 'Using Objects of Obsession as Token Reinforcers for Children with Autism.' *Journal of Autism and Developmental Disorders 28*, 3, 189–198.

CNN Interactive (1998) *Researcher Challenges when Children Should Read.* Retrieved October 20, 2004 from http://www.cnn.com/books/news/9803/02/reading.baby.cnn.

Doman, G. and Doman, J. (2002) *How to Teach Your Baby to Read.* Wyndmoor, PA: Gentle Revolution Press.

Freeman, S., Dake, L., and Tamir, I. (1997) *Teach Me Language: A Language Manual for Children with Autism, Asperger's Syndrome and Related Developmental Disorders.* Lynden, WA: Skf Books.

Fry, E., Kress, J., and Fountoukidis, D. (2000) *The Reading Teacher's Book of Lists.* San Francisco, CA: Jossey-Bass.

Grigorenko, E.L., Klin, A., and Volkmar, F. (2003) 'Annotation: Hyperlexia: Disability or Superability?' *Journal of Child Psychology and Psychiatry and Allied Disciplines 44*, 8, 1079–1091.

Gross, J. (2004) 'For Siblings of the Autistic, a Burdened Youth.' *The New York Times.* Retrieved December 14, 2004 from http://www.nytimes.com/2004/12/10/health/10siblings.html?oref=regi.

Hawley, T. (2000) 'Starting Smart.' *Ounce of Prevention Fund and ZERO TO THREE.* Retrieved October 20, 2004 from http://www.zerotothree.org/startingsmart.pdf.

Infant Learning Company (1997) *Your Baby Can Read!* Retrieved October 20, 2004 from http://www.infantlearning.com/.

KidSource OnLine, Inc. (1998) *Brain Development Research.* Retrieved October 20, 2004 from http://www.kidsource.com/kidsource/content4/brain.development.html.

Kovach, R.M. (1999) *Hannah's Hope.* Grover Beach, CA: West Wing Publishing.

Lovaas, I. (1987) 'Behavioral Treatment and Normal Educational and Intellectual Functioning in Young Autistic Children.' *Journal of Consulting and Clinical Psychology 55,* 1, 3–9.

Lovaas, I. and Smith, T. 'Early and Intensive Behavioral Intervention in Autism.' In A.E. Kazdin (ed) *Evidence-Based Psychotherapies for Children and Adolescents.* New York: Guilford Press.

One Hundred Fifth Congress of the United States of America (1997) *Individuals with Disabilities Education Act.* Retrieved December 18, 2004 from http://www.cec. sped.org/law_res/doc/law/law/index.php.

Partington, J.W. and Sundberg, M.L. (1998) *The Assessment of Basic Language and Learning Skills (the ABLLS): An Assessment, Curriculum Guide, and Skills Tracking System for Children with Autism and Developmental Disabilities.* The ABLLS Protocol. Behavior Analysis, Version 2.3 edition.

Silberberg, N. and Silberberg, M. (1967) 'Hyperlexia-Specific Word Recognition Skills in Young Children.' *Exceptional Children 5,* 3, 233–267.

Skinner, B.F. (1998) 'The Experimental Analysis of Operant Behavior: A Histroy.' In R.W. Rieber and K. Salzinger (eds) *Psychology: Theoretical-Historical Perspectives,* 2nd edition. Washington, DC: American Psychological Association.

Treffert, D.A. (2002) *Hyperlexia: Reading Precociousness or Savant Skill?* Retrieved October 20, 2004, from http://www.wisconsinmedicalsociety.org/savant/ hyperlexia.cfm.

United States Congress (1973) 'Section 504 of the Rehabilitation Act.' *1973 Rehabilitation Act.* Retrieved December 11, 2004 from http://www.ed.gov/policy/ speced/leg/rehabact.doc.

United States District Court of Maryland (1994) 'Gerstmyer vs. Howard County Public Schools 850, F. Supp. 361, 20 IDELR 1327.' *Wrightslaw.* Retrieved October 14, 2004 from http://www.wrightslaw.com/law/caselaw/case_Gerstmyer_MD_94.html.

Subject Index

Note: Page numbers in **bold** refer to diagrams and photographs.

Author Index